SHAPING THE CHURCH

Malcolm O. Tolbert

Shaping the Church

Adapting New Testament Models for Today

SMYTH & HELWYS
PUBLISHING, INCORPORATED MACON, GEORGIA

Smyth & Helwys Publishing, Inc.
6316 Peake Road
Macon, Georgia 31210-3960
1-800-747-3016

Printed in the United States of America.

The paper used in this publication meets the minimum requirements of
American National Standard for Information Sciences—
Permanence of Paper for Printed Library Materials.
ANSI Z39.48–1984. (alk. paper)

Library of Congress Cataloging-in-Publication Data

Tolbert, Malcolm.
Shaping the church : adapting New Testament church models for today /
Malcolm Tolbert.
p. cm.
ISBN 1-57312-408-7 (alk. paper)
1. Church.
2. Church—Biblical teaching.
3. Bible. N.T.—Criticism,
interpretation, etc.
I. Title.
BV600.3 .T64 2003
262—dc21

2002152734

Contents

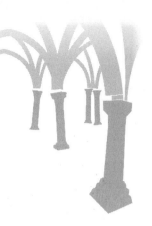

Foreword

Many churches, including the one in which I was reared, are confident that they faithfully represent the New Testament church in today's world. When we examine the New Testament carefully, however, we find that we cannot know how any church in the earliest period of Christian history functioned or was organized. We may rest assured that modern churches would be viewed as strange organizations by any early Christians transported into our times.

I do not claim that all the ideas presented in this book are original. However, I believe I do present conclusions that differ from those generally accepted by church members. Also, I shall discuss certain matters that I have not personally seen discussed anywhere else, particularly from the point of view of discovering how what we do and believe may be related to the New Testament. I refer to subjects like church buildings, frequency of worship, financial support of pastors, and others. Furthermore, I address issues that I believe are relevant to Christian churches today.

Throughout this book, we examine various aspects of church life in New Testament times to determine what we can accurately say about early churches. This is not intended as an exhaustive study of New Testament ecclesiology (the doctrine of the church). Rather, I have written about subjects concerning which I feel I had something different to say. Another consideration is important to me. I have written something that I think Christians who are interested in *being church* can read and understand.

As you read, you will sense various issues to which I am personally committed. One of my principal interests is the unity of the church. Along with my good friend Fisher Humphreys, I believe the Bible is about God's purpose to create a people who love God and love one another. I decry not only the tensions and divisions that arise in individual churches, but also the divisions that exist in Christianity as a whole. Much of our accepted ecclesiology, especially our arrogant assumption that we are right and everybody else is wrong, contributes to those divisions. I am interested in Christians being good Christians, which means they are loving people. I am interested in churches being good churches, which means they are loving communities. I am interested in individual churches having the same boundaries that God's church has. Martin Niemoeller once said to me in a conversation that when the sword fell in Nazi Germany, it cut across all denominational boundaries. The courageous members of the Confessing Church came from various denominations. In the time of crisis the real church was revealed, and it was neither Catholic nor Lutheran nor Baptist. It was God's church. That church, whose boundaries are indiscernible in ordinary times, is the only church there is. Denominational and ecclesiastical boundaries are irrelevant in determining the shape of God's church.

I have been extremely blessed in relationships with a marvelous family and great friends. My greatest blessing became a reality fifty-eight years ago when Nell Sills became my wife. Because she is afflicted with Alzheimer's, she will hardly be aware of it, but I dedicate this small volume to her as an expression of my love for her.

In conclusion, I want to express my heartfelt thanks to friends who have encouraged me, who have read all or parts of what I have written, and who have offered helpful advice with regard to ideas and diction. My gratitude especially goes out to Ellen Bandsma, one of our daughters, Dorothy Bankston, a friend since childhood, Walter Shurden, a friend from our New Orelans days together beginning in 1960, Fisher Humphreys, a former New Orleans Seminary colleague and wonderful friend, Robert Culpepper, a friend and former colleague, and Alan Neely, my companion in the wonderful and difficult days at Southeastern Seminary and since.

The New Testament Church: One "True" Church?

In my youth, I was sure that only one church rightly deserved to be called a New Testament church. That was my church, a Baptist church—or, better, a *Southern Baptist* church. This was what my grandmother—a wonderful Christian and the greatest religious influence on my life—told me. All the pastors who served our church affirmed her position. The major literary proponent of this view was *The Trail of Blood*, a pamphlet written by J. M. Carroll and published posthumously. A wide audience eagerly read this propagandistic work of historical fiction. It contributed to the exclusiveness of many Baptist churches, much of which continues today. When our church celebrated the Lord's Supper, for instance, the elements were offered only to people "of like faith and order"—in other words, other Baptists. Some churches were even more restrictive. They interpreted *church* to mean the local church only and restricted the Supper to their own members.

Baptists convinced that theirs is the only true church find the New Testament point of departure in Matthew 16:18. Jesus himself promises that the "gates of Hell" (King James Version) will not prevail against his church. The line of argument is coherent, provided you accept the assumptions. Jesus himself established the church and guaranteed its existence through the centuries until the end of time. Thus it follows that there must be a true church that has existed through the ages. Otherwise, the promise of Jesus is meaningless. However, churches and/or denominations differ from one another. This means that only one of them qualifies as the true church. The church Jesus established must resemble the church we see in the New Testament and must have existed in every age. Carroll wrote *The Trail of Blood* to prove that only the Baptist church met these qualifications. It was the only church whose characteristics corresponded to those found in the New Testament church, and it had existed since Jesus founded it.

It is true that the early churches, now called Baptist, were identified by other names in the past, but an examination of their practices showed that they possessed all the characteristics necessary to be the true church. They were Baptists in practice and beliefs if not in name. In the process, many groups were classified as Baptists that under no condition would be acceptable to Baptist churches today. The result is a view of succession that rivals that of the Roman Catholic Church. This succession of true churches stretched back in an unbroken line that began with the first true, Baptist church established by Jesus himself! I was a member of the only true church, defined as a local body of genuine Baptists. Other denominations that called themselves churches were in fact only religious societies. People in those groups had to become Baptists in order to be in the fold of the Lord.

A PREPOSTEROUS CLAIM

I did not need an extensive introduction to church history to begin to understand that this claim was preposterous and evidence had been greatly twisted in order to make it. My church was not the only one to believe that they were the sole genuine Christian church. More than one denomination has made similar claims and asserted that it alone was the real church brought into being by Christ. I have given my own academic life largely to the study of the New Testament and to the attempt to teach it. Through the years, the absurdity of the idea that anyone knows what the churches reflected in the New Testament actually looked like became increasingly clear.

We have more firsthand information about the church in Corinth than about any other church. Many unresolved questions are raised even about the issues actually treated in 1 and 2 Corinthians. For example, exactly how was the Lord's Supper observed? Why was speaking in tongues an issue in the church? Exactly what view of the resurrection was taught in the church?

In addition, there is much about which we know nothing or next to nothing because the letter is silent on some matters. How was the church governed? How did it reach decisions? How was authority defined in the church? What was the shape of its ministry? How did new Christians learn about the tenets of the faith they had recently embraced? To what extent were they acquainted with the Hebrew Bible? To what kind of catechism, if any, were they subjected? In fact, there is little we actually know about the beliefs, daily life, and religious activities of the congregation.

Any critical study of the New Testament leads to the assumption that church life, with its many aspects, varied from region to region. Whether we are conscious of it or not, culture always plays an important role in the life of the church in a given community. We cannot completely escape the influence of our culture. The ideas, practices, and institutions of the communities in which early churches were born caused churches in one place to be different from those in another.

Reading in Acts about the Jewish congregation in Jerusalem and reading the Corinthian correspondence about the Gentile congregation in Corinth, we have to believe that practices and beliefs varied widely between the two communities. The variety reflected in the New Testament documents probably accounts to some degree for the fact that, for example, the three dominant forms of church governance—congregational, presbyterian, and episcopalian—can be defended by citing legitimate proof texts in the New Testament. I have often said that I am willing to concede the possibility that the congregation in Jerusalem was Presbyterian and that the church in Ephesus was Methodist. However, I know beyond a doubt that the church in Corinth was Baptist. No church could have become so divided and flawed if there had been an ecclesiastical authority to tell it what to do and believe.

What I have said about church government applies to many other ideas and practices about which contemporary churches disagree and for which they find proof texts in the New Testament. Generally speaking, churches are not willing to admit they are doing something that is not at least tacitly sanctioned by the practices and beliefs of the early apostles and churches. In truth, often a belief, practice, or institution becomes a part of the church's life for pragmatic or traditional reasons, quite apart from any biblical origin. Once that happens, the search is on for biblical justification. This has led to creative interpretations of biblical texts in the attempt to prove that the practice or institution is actually based on the teaching of Scripture.

One of the essential, basic tenets of biblical theology is that one cannot universalize from proof texts—one of the more egregious practices of Christian communities. This caution becomes necessary especially for proof texts like the reference in 1 Corinthians 15:29 to baptism on behalf of the dead. No one knows why Paul raised the question or what the practice was. Nor can we discern whether Paul had a positive or negative reaction to the practice (whatever it was) to which he referred. Whatever the case, to infer that the practice of baptizing on behalf of the dead was universal in the churches and is essential for a genuine church today is absurd.

Having said this, however, we who are followers of Jesus today cannot escape the necessity of examining the New Testament. We must hold our beliefs and practices up to whatever light comes from those earliest Christian documents and attempt to use it as a corrective to our understanding of the Christian life. Rightly used, the Bible does not give us information in order that we may qualify as judges of others. Neither should we use it to bolster our arguments with other Christians or to demolish the ideas and practices of others with whom we disagree. Rather it is a mirror in which we see our weaknesses and strengths. Admittedly, we often see only "puzzling reflections" (1 Cor 13:12) in this mirror, an aspect of the human situation that the apostle knew we could not transcend in this life. That, however, does not absolve us of responsibility to use what we can know and understand.

THE CENTER: TRUST IN JESUS

One of the major problems of the churches with which I am most familiar is our reactionary theology. A theology formed to negate or destroy another's position can be right only by coincidence. Indeed, positions formed in the heated debates characteristic of much of Christian history often go to an extreme in the opposite direction from the opponent. Many times, the truth lies somewhere between the two extremes. The following discussions give concrete examples of this problem. My conviction is that only through our humility and love can we allow the New Testament to speak to us.

Of course, we can say with a great deal of assurance that certain aspects of the New Testament churches are clear. Most important of all, early Christians were united in their belief that Jesus rose from the dead and in their trust in him as their Savior and Lord. This faith was the common denominator amid their differences. It is still the faith that transcends individual and denominational differences and binds us together in a relationship more important than what separates us.

Early Christians felt a common need to explore the dimensions of their shared faith, to understand it better, and to translate it into the lives they were called to live in their various communities. The New

Testament is an exciting witness to that search. Each author wrote with the questions, problem, failures, and practices of a certain defined group of Christians in mind. As we study their words, we witness theology in the making as the churches confronted the pressures and questions of their world and attempted to respond in the light of their faith. Pauline studies have always appealed to me for this reason. In 1 Corinthians, for example, we see a church beset by new questions that arose from the context of the pagan environment of Corinth. Many of the questions were not—indeed, could not have been—raised in the Jewish environment of Jesus and the earliest Christians. Paul's writing is an exercise in practical theology as he tries to help the Corinthian believers come to grips with their specific questions and practices. His theology is dynamic—in the process of forming.

Someone has said that this was the only truly creative period in Christian theology, one in which theology was formed vis-à-vis the pagan world. Since that time, theology has often resulted from theological arguments among Christians, all of whom are thoroughly convinced that they are right and the other party is heretical. As we examine these controversies, in many cases they seem to involve splitting fine hairs, often with drastic consequences for the losing side. However correct and orthodox the arguments may have been on occasion, the point is that the people lost something much more important. Christians have regarded their fellow Christians as enemies instead of brothers and sisters. As a result, those brothers and sisters have been excluded, excoriated, and often severely persecuted.

In addition to their shared faith, there were also common elements in the life of New Testament churches. We can assume that activities like proclamation, evangelism, missions, and religious education were generally a part of that life. However, we cannot accurately say what form these activities took. Our churches still attempt to carry on the same kinds of activities, which we also consider indispensable. We have our Sunday schools, our seminaries, our missions organizations—none of which could have existed in the New Testament churches as they are today. Whatever the forms, however, these same areas were deemed important in the life of the early churches.

AN ENCOURAGING WORD

I think Christians are often intimidated by what they perceive as their vast ignorance of the Bible. To counter that, I have often stated that good Christians in every age have known everything they needed to know to be good followers of Jesus Christ. In Bible conferences over the years, I stated repeatedly that the most important things I would say were not new to my audience. Rather, they were what my audience already knew. In other words, the people and the Bible teacher were on the same level in terms of the most important issues of the Christian faith.

For many centuries, most Christians did not even possess a copy of Scripture, and many were unable to read. My grandmother was one of these Christians. She was unacquainted with Christian history other than the distorted one she learned at church. She knew nothing about the Greek New Testament. She had the King James Bible and knew nothing about its antecedents or the state of textual criticism today. I know more about the New Testament than she could have possibly known. But she knew God better than I do. She knew the really important things because she was loving, forgiving, kind, and generous. Her limited resources in literature and education did not limit her understanding of what it meant to be a good follower of Jesus. She was responsive to the Spirit of God as God spoke to her through her Christian community, her King James Bible, and her prayers.

Again, there is much we cannot learn about the earliest churches, much no scholar will ever uncover. Nevertheless, what is true of good Christians and the Bible is also true about churches and the Bible. Everything we need to know in order to be a good church is accessible to us. As with our failures in Christian living, our problem is not our lack of knowledge. Our problem is that we do not respond to what is available to us. We do not do what we know to do. If we simply attempted to measure our congregational life according to what we learn in Ephesians 4 alone, for example, we could experience a tremendous transformation in who we are. The New Testament is more than adequate as individual congregations attempt to become what the Lord of the church intends that we become.

Measured by the New Testament yardstick, there are good churches that differ widely in organization and practice. The question is not the titles given to individual ministers or the definitions of their roles. The question is whether these ministers measure up to the clear standard for ministry that exists in the New Testament, which we shall discuss in a later chapter. The question is not how your boards and committees are formed. The question is how the church organizations function to help you achieve the ideal of loving God with the totality of your being and loving your neighbor as yourself.

THE IDOLATRY OF FORM

As I have indicated, the New Testament raises more questions than it gives answers as we try to understand the way churches functioned in the earliest days. Questions can be a blessing because we are so prone to the idolatry of form. An example comes from my own religious background. Baptist churches in the South commonly had morning and evening services on Sundays. This probably was due to several factors. One would be the agricultural background of the churches. In my earlier days, people who farmed were more likely to attend the evening service than the morning worship. Also, the church was the center of social life. Boys and girls could get together at church—one of the main reasons the organization called Baptist Young People's Union, which met on Sunday evenings, was so well supported in the thirties and forties.

However, life in the United States, both north and south, has changed radically in my generation. Generally, only a small percentage of people attend evening church gatherings. Those who do attend are often the most faithful members, the ones who need it the least. Yet some churches apparently believe that canceling the evening service would betray their loyalty to Jesus Christ. This attitude exists in spite of the fact that the Bible does not indicate how often churches in New Testament times came together on Sunday or, for that matter, during the week. The truth is that we do not have to go to the church building twice on Sunday to be good Christians. The preachers in southern churches that still cling to fifty-year-old patterns are asked to do what few human beings are capable of doing—prepare two creative sermons a week and deliver them well on Sunday.

Churches tend to cling to forms even when they no longer serve a real purpose in helping the church become the church in our day. Of course, we can see many egregious examples of this idolatry of form in the history of every denomination. We should constantly give healthy criticism to the forms of our church life, asking, "Are these forms adequate to contain the wine of the gospel in this day?" That is the real question. How well do our practices and institutions carry on the preaching, teaching, evangelism, and other activities important to churches from the beginning? Therefore, knowing exactly what forms early churches adopted would hinder our ministry. The forms of early churches were more or less adequate for their day. However, they would be totally inadequate for churches in our world today. Churches whose lives were shaped by first-century forms would be anachronistic in the contemporary world.

The Importance of the Church

The Bible is a revelation of God's activity in history, helping us begin to comprehend the purpose of God's work throughout the centuries. I can summarize that *God's purpose in history has been to create a people who live in community who love God and love one another.*[1] That has been the central goal of God's activity through the centuries.

THE TEACHING OF JESUS

A statement of Jesus gives a good biblical proof text for God's purpose: "'You shall love the Lord your God with all your heart, and with all your soul, and with all your mind.' This is the greatest and first commandment. And a second is like it: 'You shall love your neighbor as yourself.' *On these two commandments hang all the law and the prophets*" (Matt 22:37-40, my italics). The last part of that statement is extremely important, for it explains Jesus' method of dealing with the Law from the perspective of Matthew's Gospel. As the greatest commandments of all, the two Jesus quoted determined how people were to interpret every other commandment.

In Matthew 5:21-48, for example, Jesus reinterpreted six commandments found in the law. In none of the six examples did he take the legalistic approach dominant in his day. When love is the guiding criterion, religion becomes a matter of the heart and legalism becomes impossible. In New Testament vocabulary the heart is the center of the inner life of humans, the seat of will, resolve, and understanding. Thus, the depth and reality of our commitment to God or our attitude toward others is hidden from human view. It is no longer something we can measure adequately by using the fulfillment of a code of conduct as a standard. If murder and adultery are now considered attitudes of the heart and not simply outward acts, only God can know the murderers and adulterers who do not act overtly. An individual may be moral in act but immoral in the heart, and the heart is not subject to our inspection. According to Jesus' teaching, in order to qualify as a righteous act, what one does must arise out of love, the guiding dynamic at the center of one's being.[2]

Furthermore, in two of the six examples Jesus used in Matthew 5 to illustrate how the law of love affects the interpretation of other laws, he did not reinterpret and deepen the Old Testament commandments. He set the Old Testament laws aside altogether, taking the position that to live by them was contrary to the law of love (Matt 5:33, 38). To shape one's conduct by those laws would bring one into conflict with loving action. This was a cavalier and shocking approach to the law for first-century Jews who believed that the whole of the law should be observed. Obviously, Jesus was not a biblical literalist. Rather, as all of us do whether we admit it or not, he interpreted the Bible from a certain perspective. He chose love instead of holiness or sovereignty, for example, as the key to interpreting the purpose and actions of God.

From the perspective of first-century Judaism, Jesus threatened to undermine the whole religious system based on the fulfillment of the laws of the Old Testament *as interpreted by the rabbis*. Jesus was a radical in the first century. He is still a radical if we understand him correctly. According to his teaching, when we act in any situation with our love for God and for another person as our focus, we have done everything that God wants us to do. That is true today. It has always been true. This concept should be of central importance for the way we read and interpret both the Old and New Testaments.

THE DESTRUCTION OF COMMUNITY

If the position expressed by Jesus is correct, God desires to create community. Furthermore, God's actions in history are directed toward securing the fulfillment of that desire. On the other hand, more often than not the actions of human beings have led to alienation from God and their neighbors. The book of Genesis paints a vivid picture of this problem. First, human beings were alienated from God, given over to their own choice to live independently from the Creator, victims of the ever-recurring pride that makes people want to be gods. They were driven from Eden where they had lived in fellowship with God.

The consequences of the human attempt to wrest control of their lives from the hands of God soon became apparent. Alienation from God resulted in alienation among human beings. Cain killed Abel. When we forget our real Parent, we do not recognize our brother or sister. Tragically and prophetically, the cause of the first murder is connected to the different ways two individuals worshiped God. That sin has been replicated in exactly the same way through the centuries, often with the same deadly consequence. How many lives have been destroyed because of differences among people in worship and belief?

Other stories follow in the wake of this first murder. Genesis 6:1ff. presents a story of complete corruption. The only description of the corruption is found in the phrase "the earth is filled with violence," implying that there was unrestrained anarchy and chaos—the kind of situation that becomes characteristic of our world when hatred and prejudice are the rule rather than the exception.

Just after the story of Noah and the flood appears the interesting account of the tower of Babel (Gen 11:1ff.) Human beings attempted to overcome their alienation from one another and the insecurity of their godless lives by uniting behind a project. They proposed to construct a building in order to make a name for themselves, that is, establish their identity. They did not know who they really were—the children of the living God. God's children have no cause for insecurity. They do not need to make a name for themselves. They are not driven to feverish acts of dominance and pride to prove they are somebody. They are children of the living God, and no human status can equal that.

The story of Babel is the story of so much that has happened in human history. Human beings, attempting to make a name for ourselves, have constructed marvelous buildings through the ages. In the effort to create community and overcome alienation from our fellows, we attempt to enlist others behind a project. Rather than create community, however, we often create the opposite. In some form or another, this story has repeated itself numerous times. Isolated from God, the true source of community, such attempts often end in the dissolution of community.

Those of us involved in work with churches have witnessed tragic divisions that resulted from disagreements about the building being constructed, sometimes about issues as banal as which carpet color to use. According to the story, the efforts of the people of Babel ended in frustration. As a result of the attempt to make a name for themselves, they became completely alienated from their fellows, and their building project ended in disaster. The result was that they could no longer understand one another. The friend became the enemy, someone to be feared, a member of another tribe. Communication was no longer possible. Or, as Genesis expresses it in the shorthand characteristic of the Old Testament, God confused their language and scattered them abroad. In the insecurity we have created, we build walls around our cities, engage in armament races, and take other destructive measures that tend to produce the opposite of what we want. The human story often ends with a sad epitaph: "Seeking to save themselves, they have destroyed themselves."

GOD REFUSES TO WITHDRAW

In Genesis, nevertheless, we soon realize that God did not withdraw from the scene and that the purpose of the Creator still lived. God was determined to have a people who loved God and loved one another, and human evil would not be allowed to frustrate that purpose. That is what the call of Abraham is about. God chose Abraham to be the instrument of a new beginning to achieve God's purpose. There is a great unsolvable mystery in this story. Why does God choose a certain person? Is that choice dependent on an individual's superior moral qualities? The stories about Abraham, a flawed individual, are enough to show us that is not the case. Is the choice dependent on the individual's openness to the call of God? Had God attempted to work in lives of people other than Abraham who were unmoved by those efforts? We do not find answers in the account, nor are we likely to find them elsewhere. Suffice it to say that through the centuries individuals have had the strange, ineluctable conviction that God has laid a hand upon them, giving them a special role to fulfill, and they have been compelled to acquiesce to that choice.

One of the main lessons from the story of Abraham is that election not only confers privilege; it also places awesome responsibilities on the chosen ones. The primary purpose of God is not achieved with the choice of an individual. God chooses individuals in order that they may become instruments in the divine enterprise to create a people who love God and love each other. This truth has not always been understood. As a result, too often people who believed God chose them have responded to that call with smugness and arrogance. They consider themselves one of the "elect," a member of God's favored minority, somehow superior to all others. Arrogance is the primary sin of human beings, and spiritual arrogance is the worst kind of all. The account tells us that Abraham was the beginning rather than the ultimate point of God's redemption. Though fallible and sinful, he was an important beginning that led to a multitude of descendants, a great people united to each other as the consequence of their relationship to God.

THE SAGA OF ISRAEL'S REDEMPTION

As we follow the story, we witness Abraham's descendants suffer in abject slavery. The natural assumption would be that God's efforts to create a people through Abraham had failed dismally. Anybody who heard the story of God's promise to Abraham would have burst into derisive laughter in light of that development. The question may well have arisen: Will God, apparently defeated in the attempt to create a people of the descendants of Abraham, abandon this pathetic bunch of slaves and look for a more promising nucleus for a people? Would God choose, as humans would, from the high and powerful of the world?

As it turns out, that was not even a consideration. Thus, the stage was set for a critical revelation. God would redeem this bunch of slaves. God's people would be created out of those with nothing to commend themselves, who were on the bottom of humanity's social hierarchy, a helpless mass of slaves. They would be created in the way that God always creates a people—by redeeming them from their slavery. There is no room for pride in the individual who recognizes this incredible truth. All that we are and hope to be is due to the awesome and powerful redeeming grace of God. We are God's people because, and only because, the God who created us also loves us with an incredible love.

The saga of Israel's redemption is found in Exodus. My Old Testament colleagues often began their study of the Old Testament with Exodus in order to pinpoint its pivotal significance in Israel's story. The faith expressed in the book of Genesis cannot be explained apart from the people whose redemption is described in Exodus. Through the centuries, over and over again, prophets called Israel back to God by reminding them of the story of Exodus—of what God did for their ancestors when they were totally helpless, how God created a people out of nobodies.

Once again, a person was chosen to be the human instrument of God's redemptive purpose. Like so many people confronted with the awesome call of God, Moses struggled with his own limitations.

Even so, he found confidence, as do all genuine servants of God, in the assurance that the God who called him would provide the resources needed to respond to that call. Under the leadership of Moses, the people were led from captivity into the desert, the place lacking in water and food where they were totally dependent on the care of God.

A COVENANT RELATIONSHIP

In the desert God entered into a covenant with a redeemed people. In the covenant God gave them the assurance that the people of God always need: God would be with them; they would never be forsaken. They could always depend on their Redeemer. Faithfulness to relationships is central to the character of God. Above all else, we can depend on God. This is one of the primary meanings of the biblical term "righteousness" when applied to human beings as well as God. Ultimately, the righteous person is faithful in relationships. Righteous people can be counted on to do what they pledge to do. Their spouses, their children, their associates, and their friends can trust them implicitly.

Therefore God, the righteous God, was bound to the people in a covenant that was a pledge of faithfulness to them. Furthermore, God called on them to be righteous, faithful in their relationship to the one who redeemed them. What that means is set forth in what we call the Law. It is generally recognized that the center of the law is found in the Decalogue or the Ten Commandments.[3] The Decalogue is divided into two parts. The first part describes what it means to be faithful to God and the second what it means to be faithful in community. God and community—these are two sides of the same reality. A relationship with God always involves a relationship with God's people. God's purpose in history is to overcome the alienation that afflicts humanity by redeeming the alienated and, in so doing, to reconcile them to one another.

THE MINISTRY OF THE PROPHETS

The story of redemption is about God's unwavering faithfulness to the people despite their repeated failures to respond to that faithfulness. Many of the Old Testament books called the Prophets were written in protest against sins that related to the two aspects of the redeemed person's relationship as set forth in the law. More often than not, Israel failed to live up to the divine reality of her life. She was often driven by the pervasive tendency to be like her pagan neighbors. Cultural pressure to conform, to be accepted, to be powerful was as difficult to resist then as it is now. The people of Israel often fell into idolatry, worshiping the gods of their neighbors. Nothing is truly new. To be in the world but not become a part of the world is the constant challenge facing God's people.

Also, the temptation was always present for the rich and powerful to use, exploit, and mistreat their sisters and brothers, often covering their abuse with an ostentatious attention to trappings of the cult, such as the temple ritual of burnt offerings and sacrifices. The first chapter of Isaiah offers an illustration. First of all, Isaiah excoriated the people for their rebellion against God. Outwardly they were religious, bringing offerings, burning incense, and observing new moons and sabbaths (Isa 1:11ff.). Worship, however, is acceptable only when it arises from the life of a person seeking to live as a child of God. What does that mean? It means that you love people, especially the most helpless people of the community. That is the unavoidable message of the great prophets.

Love in the Bible is not an emotion; rather, love is action that has as its goal the welfare of the person loved. Isaiah implored the people: "learn to do good; seek justice, rescue the oppressed, defend the orphan, plead for the widow" (1:17). All human societies tolerate the neglect, mistreatment, exploitation, and abuse of the poor. Some societies are somewhat more just than others, but none is without this grievous problem. In contrast, a salient aspect of the goodness of God is concern for the poor and helpless. Perhaps the clearest message of the prophets is that God is on the side of the poor! Those who are truly God's people, therefore, regard the poor in the same way God does. The prophets interpret failure to meet the needs of the poor as an act of rebellion against God. It is the failure to live up to one's responsibility and calling as a member of God's redeemed community.

Many of the prophets express the burden of Isaiah 1. One of Israel's primary problems was the tendency to forget that she had been a slave people who owed her existence to the powerful grace of God. Those who are sufficiently aware of God's grace and sufficiently thankful for it can never arrogantly isolate themselves and their wealth from others whom God also loves. Primary in the divine purpose is God's desire to love excluded people through the community that God created.

It is clear, therefore, that in the Old Testament love for God and love for others are bound inextricably together. God intends to create a community. Any action that weakens the community is an act of rebellion against God. Moreover, all selfish acts by a single member of the community weaken it. "Lone-ranger religion" does not exist in the Old Testament. True religion is that which guides the life of the individual in community. Community is always the context of every action, and every action is under the judgment of God in terms of the welfare of the community. Admittedly, the true followers of God in the Old Testament were often a painful minority, sometimes represented in the person of a lone prophet. But the prophets were always in the service of God, and they directed their ministry toward creating and maintaining community.

JESUS AND COMMUNITY

What about the New Testament? Contrary to much popular religion with its emphasis on the individual, the same purpose that we have seen in the Old Testament is central to the New. Many have argued the question of how Jesus understood himself and his ministry. New Testament writers depict him as prophet, priest, king, savior. Any one of these images helps us focus on one aspect of Jesus' ministry. He was certainly depicted as a prophet in various places, and, like the prophets, he directed his ministry toward Israel. Like them, he believed that Israel was in rebellion against God, and that rebellion showed in the way certain people were excluded from the approved circle. Jesus spent his entire ministry serving God to help achieve the purpose of creating a people who love God and love one another. Story after story in the Gospels tell us how Jesus included the excluded, loved the unloved, and ministered to the neglected in the service of God. The parables in Luke 15 are powerful illustrations of that fact.

Many scholars have questioned whether or not Jesus intended to begin a community. One piece of evidence used to illustrate Jesus' intention in this regard is his choice of the Twelve. They represented the redeemed Israel, the holy remnant, the people of God. Interestingly, the New Testament books tell us little about most of the Twelve, leaving a yawning gap to be filled by tradition, often with stories that no doubt have little foundation in fact.[4] If what is preserved in our records comes close to giving us a true picture, the story of their lives was not a central focus of New Testament communities. On the other hand, the number twelve was apparently very significant. This is shown, for example, by the fact that the apostles felt it necessary to have one selected by the community to replace Judas (Acts 1:15 ff.).[5] They wanted to preserve the number twelve, a witness to Jesus' primary concern about community—a community that continued what God had been doing through centuries past.

In this regard, the incident recorded in Matthew 16:13-20, popularly known as the Great Confession, is important. Peter confessed Jesus as the Messiah. The story tells us that Jesus exulted because of that insight and immediately exclaimed: "On this rock I will build my church." We see, therefore, that Peter's "personal profession of faith" was not the goal of Jesus' ministry. Certainly it was important, but it was important because it enabled Jesus to begin doing what he had come to do—to build his church. One person saw the light. One person expressed his faith. However imperfect, fragile, and limited that faith might have been, it was enough to serve as the beginning of something much larger. It was the initial human stone for the building of the new temple, God's new community—the church.

A FLAWED EVANGELISM

One of the major weaknesses of many evangelical Christians is that they see the "salvation of souls" as the fulfillment of Jesus' purpose. While I taught in a seminary, an evangelistic conference was in progress whose focus was primarily the evangelization of individuals. One of the men attending that conference came up to me and asked, "Brother, are you saved?" My first reaction was anger. I was angry because the question indicated that he did not care about me as a person. I was an object—a possible conquest in his campaign for souls. He was not concerned with whether I was in the midst of dealing with tragedy, suffered from some serious illness, or had experienced severe disappointment in my life. His perception of me was flat, without any depth whatsoever. I was what he considered a "prospect," which is a harsh, impersonal, self-serving description current in evangelical circles. I was a possible scalp to display proudly on his soul-winners belt, a statistic to boast about in the next meeting of his group. If he had been able to "win me to Christ," that would have been the end of his relationship with me. I would have been saved from hell and on my way to heaven. The interesting aspect of this encounter was that it would have been so easy to satisfy the man. All it took was one word: "Yes." If I had said that word, he would have gone on to the next "prospect." Or if I had said, "No," he was prepared to deal with that.

After all, he had memorized the "Roman road to salvation." Little did he realize that Paul himself had not done any of those things demanded in the "plan of salvation" prior to becoming a Christian.

This man's approach, and that of many evangelical Christians today, contrasts sharply with what we read about the way Jesus related to people in the New Testament. He was concerned about them as individuals. He related to each one in a different way, a way that shows his sensitivity to people. He did not approach people with a standardized question. For example, in his relationship to Zacchaeus (Luke 19:1-10), he had no question and no condemnation. Rather, he opened his arms in unconditional acceptance by telling Zacchaeus he was going to eat with him.[6]

Furthermore, Jesus' purpose was to bring people into a loving, caring, supportive community. The Gospel of John emphasizes this purpose in statements like the one found in John 13:34: "I give you a new commandment, that you love one another. Just as I have loved you, you also should love one another." Those who evangelize ignore the biblical model if they do not look beyond the conversion of the individual to the integration of that individual into God's redeemed and loving community.

PAUL'S EMPHASIS ON UNITY

The relationship of Christians to one another was of primary importance to Paul, as we clearly see in an examination of his letters. In sections of the letters where he gave instructions to guide believers in their Christian living, more often than not the need for unity was the first item on his agenda. How the people lived together and related to one another in God's community went to the very heart of the gospel. In 1 Corinthians, for example, Paul addressed division in the church first. From our reading of the letter, we know that the church in Corinth faced many problems and issues. For Paul, however, none was as important as the fellowship of the community. Evidently, the people of the church supported outstanding preachers who had become cult figures or gurus, a phenomenon that has always divided the church. Only after dealing with that fundamental rupturing of fellowship did Paul turn to other important issues and questions (1 Cor 1:10 ff.).

When Paul finished what is often called the doctrinal section of Ephesians, the first subject he turned to was the need and basis for church unity (see 4:1 ff.). In Romans 12, as Paul began to give instruction in Christian living to the Romans, he opened with a plea to the believers to make a radical commitment of themselves to God (12:1-2). After this opening plea he immediately talked about the individual in the context of the community. Even in the Epistle to the Philippians, a church very dear to Paul, he turned almost immediately to the need for the church to experience community (see 2:1 ff.). No church has developed in its fellowship to the maximum degree. There is always room for improvement in community.

Why did Paul give such a prominent place to the unity of the church? The answer is clear. He understood what God in Christ was doing. God was involved in a ministry of reconciliation, tearing down the wall that separated human beings from their Creator and from one another (Eph 2:14 ff.). To Paul a divided church contradicted the gospel. When people became Christians, the miraculous love of God for them became a power in their reconciled lives. God's love in us enables us to love one another. That is the teaching of the whole Bible rightly understood.

IMAGES OF THE CHURCH

A good many years ago Paul Minear wrote a book titled *Images of the Church in the New Testament* (Philadelphia: Westminster Press, 1960). In it he attempted to identify all the images used to depict the church, both major and minor, and discussed their significance. It is a valuable study. A large number of these images relate to our discussion. I shall mention a few of them to illustrate my point.

An important image is "the people of God," found in fourteen books of the New Testament. This phrase contains a number of significant implications. First the church is a community of people who belong to God. It is God's people, and that makes it different from any other people in the world. The expression is also used to designate Israel of the Old Testament. Its use in the New Testament accentuates the continuity between the Israel of the Old Testament and the church of the New Testament. Of course, it indicates that individuals are important as members of this people. Each has a relationship to all the others.

In Ephesians 2:20-22 we are told that the church is a building "built upon the foundation of the apostles and prophets, with Christ Jesus himself as the cornerstone. In him the whole structure is joined together and grows into a holy temple in the Lord; in whom you also are built together spiritually into a dwelling place for God." In this passage the church is a holy temple, a dwelling for God's Spirit, and its components are the individual members who serve as the stones. This is a vivid image used to illustrate the truth that God in Christ has created a community.[7]

One of the most important images of the church is "body of Christ." This image originates with Paul, who used it for the first time in 1 Corinthians (see 12:12 ff.) This was a happy image to explain what Paul wanted the divided Corinthian church to understand. Christians are all different. However, that is a good thing. The members of the human body are also different from each other, and all of us will agree that is fortunate. Each member of the body is important because another member cannot perform its function. The image of the church as body is one of the most significant found in the New Testament to emphasize the point that God's purpose in Christ is to create a community. Also, what we learn about the Corinthian church is a forceful illustration about how individuals can be a handicap to the achievement of God's purpose through their prejudice, their narrow views, their spiritual arrogance, and their lack of concern for one another.

Other images are found here and there. Perhaps you can think of some of them. Disciples constitute a flock; they are members of a family; they are citizens of a heavenly land. All these images aid one another in making the point that God is creating a community of people who love one another.

THE BIBLE: A BOOK FOR A COMMUNITY

As seen in the Great Confession passage cited earlier, the conversion of individuals is important, but it is not the fulfillment of God's purpose for them. When we turn to God in faith, we have not done what God wants us to do. Our faith simply places us in a position to begin to do what God desires. God is creating a community, and every person who comes to faith is destined by God to be an instrument in the achievement of that purpose. We could multiply references in both the Gospels and the other books of the New Testament to show that the writers of the books thought in terms of the community. All the books were written in the context of various communities to encourage the fainthearted, answer the questions, deal with the issues, and solve the problems faced by various churches in different parts of the Roman Empire. The issues, questions, and problems differed from region to region and from church to church. Nevertheless, one thing is true of all the books: they arose in the context of churches and were designed to help churches.

Indeed, the only way members of the churches could know about the documents was by being present in the assembly with their brothers and sisters when the documents were read. The people did not possess individual copies that they could read in their homes, and most of the members could not have read them even if they had had a copy. Churches became aware of the materials we read in the New Testament only as these books were read aloud during an assembly of the church.

Paul wrote his letters to be read in the church meeting.[8] Even the letter to Philemon, having to do with a matter apparently involving only one member of the church, a slave owner, was addressed also to the church and was intended for public reading. From Paul's point of view members did not have private business. Everything was set in the context of the community.

FACTORS CAUSING FRAGMENTATION OF COMMUNITY

Several factors have contributed to the modern fragmentation of Christian communities and the individualization of their members. One important influence is the context of the culture. Modern, western society places so much emphasis on the individual and is inimical to the sense of community. One of the grave difficulties people have in understanding the Bible is the totally different social context in which they live today. In Hebrew thought, the primary fact about individuals was that they belonged to a certain family, a certain tribe. Individuals were never considered in isolation. Therefore, in Old Testament times a whole tribe might receive punishment for the sins of an individual. That vastly differs from our modern juridical system in which a child can be held accountable separately and apart from an abusive family that may be more to blame than the child for the crime committed.

Understanding, therefore, that the general context in which churches find themselves contributes to the fragmentation of community, we should note that some factors peculiar to modern Christianity deserve attention. Strangely enough, one of the most important of these is the invention of the printing press, which made it possible for us to possess individual copies of Scripture to read in the privacy of our homes. We have an inescapable tendency to read the Bible as a private message to us as individuals. That is, we often do not read it with the awareness that all of it was written for a community—the Old Testament for Israel and the New Testament for churches. Not understanding that the Bible is addressed to us only as members of a community subjects us to misunderstanding the Bible's meaning. Many people think that, alone with their Bibles, they can be good Christians and live isolated from their brothers and sisters. Though this opinion contradicts the biblical perspective, many arrogantly assume that they can be better Christians apart from the church.

No doubt television also plays a large part in the fragmentation of the churches. People can sit at home, listen to and watch their favorite television preacher, and worship God without ever getting dressed to go outside the house. Further involvement, if there is any, often takes the form of a monetary gift to help the preacher continue his or her "ministry." Great stretches of the New Testament cannot apply to such isolated individuals. For example, they can do without the Sermon on the Mount where the teachings of Jesus are set in the context of the community. They can dispense with passages like Ephesians 4 and 1 Corinthians 13. If you are not in close association with your brothers and sisters, you do not need to bear with them in love, and certainly you do not need to exert any effort to "maintain the unity of the Spirit in the bond of peace" (Eph 4:3). You need not concern yourself with forgiving others since they cannot offend you if you have no contact with them.

MY RESPONSIBILITY

If the divine purpose is to create a community of people who love God and love one another, I am placed under a tremendous obligation. I need to become active in what God does in the world. The only way I know to do that is by becoming a part of a Christian community where I live. This often is difficult for us. Being involved with a church requires becoming involved with people, and people can and do test our patience. As members of a church, we must contend with the fact that our fellow members—and ourselves—are imperfect. We often do not act the way we think Christians should. We can sometimes say harsh, critical things. We often get angry if others do not see things the way we do. This kind of behavior scandalizes people and causes many to give up on the church. We must recognize, however, that those very imperfections allows us to become truly Christian.

If we relate closely to a group, we will have the opportunity to grow in the exercise of patience, to practice forgiveness, and to love in the same way that God loves. God is the prime example of one who loves imperfect people. As we all know, belonging to a church does not in and of itself guarantee that people become good Christians. However, only as participants in a community that God is creating can we receive the opportunity to become good followers of Jesus Christ. Walter Shurden drove this point home:

> It is here, in a local body of believers, where people meet eyeball to eyeball, where faces have names, where people live life with all its failures and foibles, where imperfections are acknowledged and forgiven, and where Christians really learn that we "are all the same." It is here that theological convictions regarding human depravity and divine grace become more than creedal affirmations; they become part of what Bonhoeffer called "life together." It is here—in a local church—where fragmented and frightened folk learn "to belong" to each other, and where they learn that together they belong to God.[9]

NOTES

[1] The first person I heard express the idea in exactly this way was Fisher Humphreys. We may say that one of the primary ways to love God is by loving one another. (See 1 John 4:7-12.)

[2] How do you define an act as a Christian act? In the light of the idea developed here it seems to me that we can classify only those things that are helpful as truly Christian.

[3] Exodus 20:1-17.

[4] For example, Matthias is never heard from again once he is chosen as one of the Twelve.

[5] For more, see the chapter on Pentecost.

[6] To eat with a person in the Semitic world signified to everyone else that you accepted that person. Jesus' acceptance of certain people, signified by his eating meals with them, angered his enemies.

[7] For more on this image of the church as temple, see chapter 5.

[8] The exception is the Pastorals, written to single individuals. However, the concern in those books was the churches. Most scholars believe that someone other than Paul wrote the Pastorals.

[9] Walter B. Shurden, "The Baptist Tradition of Community and the Contemporary Affliction," T. B. Maston Lectures, Carson-Newman College, 23 March 1992.

Pentecost: The Birth of the Church

In one sense we could say the church was born when God redeemed a bunch of slaves from Egypt and established a covenant relationship with them. Apparently this was Paul's view when he emphasized to the Gentiles that they had been grafted into the olive tree, that is, into Israel (Rom 11:17ff.). He had no sense that he was converting, that is, adopting a new religion. He was a Jew who became convinced that God's Messiah was Jesus of Nazareth. We can say the same of the earliest disciples who, according to the Acts account, continued their Jewish worship in the synagogue and temple. They apparently believed that their participation in Jewish worship was valid (Acts 2:46).[1] Indeed, Acts reports that Paul continued to be a practicing Jew as long as Jewish religious requirements did not conflict with his understanding of the gospel (see Acts 21:26).

From the Christian perspective, nonetheless, Jesus was the decisive, climactic point in God's redemptive activity in the world. What came into being because of him differed in many ways from what preceded his coming. The purpose God initiated with the call of Abraham—the creation of a people who love God and love each other—reached its climax in Jesus of Nazareth. Through him, the remnant was gathered and the church, the community of the end-time, came into being.[2]

The story of Jesus did not end, however, with the resurrection and ascension. The redemptive and creative ministry of Jesus had to be brought to completion. In Acts 1 and 2 Luke gives us his description of the final, essential step in the process through which God had been working to create a people.

THE PROMISED GIFT OF THE SPIRIT

According to the Lucan account, after Jesus' resurrection he appeared at various times to disciples across a period of forty days. We are told that he taught them about the kingdom, but the only specific instructions he gave them are found in Acts 1:4-5. In his ministry, John the Baptist had prophesied that a crucial, long-awaited event was about to take place. Unlike John who baptized with water, the Messiah, the bearer of the Spirit, would baptize his people with the Spirit (Matt 3:11). Stimulated by statements found in the Old Testament[3] and inspired by the hope centered in a coming Messiah, many Jews in those days of apocalyptic fervor fully expected this to happen in their lifetime. For those first followers of Jesus, the resurrection confirmed that he was indeed the long-awaited Messiah. However, some aspects of the expectations related to the coming Messiah, which they also evidently embraced as Jews, had not yet been fulfilled. The contemporary expectations of many people were based in part on passages like Joel 2:28, which promised that the Spirit would be poured out on all God's people in the last days. This had not yet taken place. However, in Acts 1:4-5 Jesus assures the disciples that what John foresaw is about to take place. The guarantee of its fulfillment was nothing less than the faithfulness of God. God had promised to pour out the Spirit upon the people of the new covenant,[4] and God always fulfilled what God promised.

Jesus' affirmation that his disciples would soon be baptized with the Spirit provoked a question—one easily understood in the light of certain first-century messianic expectations. The pouring out of the Spirit (Spirit baptism) was connected to the eschaton, the last days. At that time the kingdom—that is, the rule of God—would be established and the powers of evil would be totally defeated. Jewish people expected Israel to play a central role under that rule. In the first century, therefore, suffering under the heavy hand of Rome, many people cherished the hope that the Messiah would appear in their time. They firmly believed that, upon his coming, the Messiah would liberate them from hated Roman chains, restore Israel to its former place of glory, and fulfill the expectations of the prophets that the nations of the world would march to Mount Zion. Acts helps us understand that the nationalistic nature of the disciples' theology had not changed in spite of the time they had spent with Jesus. Their expectations about God's deliverance were largely connected to their own aspirations as Jews. According to Jesus' words, the disciples could expect that one event commonly associated with the end-time, their baptism with the Spirit, would soon take place. When that happened, they were sure that God's promise concerning the liberation of Israel would also be fulfilled. Thus their logical concerned the timing: "Lord, is this the time when you will restore the kingdom to Israel?" (Acts 1:6).

Jesus did not answer their question; instead he rejected it. "It is not for you to know the times or periods that the Father has set by his own authority," he told them (Acts 1:7). Questions about the time of the end were not appropriate for disciples. God was in charge of the future, and they were to trust God with it. Scholars have recognized that one of Luke's purposes was probably to deal with false expectations about the end-time. From Luke's point of view, speculation about the future is never appropriate for Christians (see, e.g., Luke 19:11ff.). With faith in the God of the future, we are to commit ourselves to our mission for the present, the only moment we actually have. Faith in the God of the future frees God's people from responsibility and anxiety about what may happen. It enables us to live responsibly in the present God has given us.

In spite of Luke's clear statement, thousands of people throughout the last two millennia have claimed they could do what, according to Acts, Jesus refused to do—that is, predict when God would act to bring the world to a close. Of course, the batting average of such people is zero, but even that does not dampen their enthusiasm for making predictions or the uncritical ardor of those who inevitably embrace what they predict. One aspect of apocalyptic language with its picturesque images, as found in Revelation, Daniel, and Ezekiel, is that it lends itself to fanciful interpretations. This enables people to prove widely variant and often conflicting views through their uncritical use of the Bible.

Jesus, for his part, called the attention of the disciples to the responsibility laid upon them for the moment God had given to them: "But you will receive power when the Holy Spirit has come upon you; and you will be my witnesses in Jerusalem, in all Judea and Samaria, and to the ends of the earth" (Acts 1:8). Their role was to testify to what God had already done and not to predict what God was going to do. When Jesus' followers received the Spirit, they would be equipped to begin their ministry as witnesses to the central event of all history—the life, death, and resurrection of Jesus. Notice that no conditions were set for the baptism with the Spirit. It would happen "when," not "if," the Holy Spirit came upon them.

Many people have written books about what one must do to receive the Spirit. Claiming to base their teachings on Acts, ironically in contradiction to what it really teaches, they make the possession of the Holy Spirit the result of what the believer does, not the result of the promise of God. We are given what God promises to give us. There is no explanation for this other than the faithfulness of God to those promises. In another context, Paul argues that promise and grace go together, not promise and works (e.g., Gal 3:18). The gift of the Spirit is solely a matter of grace. It is truly and totally a gift and not something the believer earns by persistence in prayers or the quality of the moral life. As Paul states in Galatians 4:6a: "*because you are children*, God has sent the Spirit of his Son into our hearts" (my italics).

The teachings about the Holy Spirit in the New Testament are many and varied, but Luke's major concern was *to connect the Holy Spirit with the world mission of the church*. Many people emphasize how the Spirit makes them feel, as though it were some kind of heavenly Valium tablet. Luke emphasized action—what disciples would do after they received the Spirit. They would begin their mission in the world. This close connection between the Spirit and the world mission of the church is one key to understanding the book of Acts.

Let us note that the only command given by the risen Jesus to the disciples was that they should wait in Jerusalem for the baptism of the Spirit. The reception of the Spirit, however, was not contingent on obedience to that command. The text makes the reason for the command clear. When the disciples received the Spirit, they would begin preaching the gospel. From Luke's point of view, the world mission of the church was to begin in Jerusalem and move from there to the uttermost reaches of the world. Since the disciples would begin their witness to Jesus with the coming of the Spirit, they needed to be in Jerusalem when that event took place in keeping with God's plan for the evangelization of the world. In this mission to the disparate peoples of the Empire, as described in Acts, the Spirit played a key role—overcoming obstacles such as deeply entrenched racial prejudice, imparting courage in a time of persecution, giving directions, and illuminating both the messenger and the recipient of the message.

A NEW SITUATION

After Jesus' departure, the disciples found themselves in a situation altogether different from any they had known since they first began to follow him. During their time with Jesus, he had been their decision-maker; he had determined the locale and shape of their ministry; he had answered their questions; he had conveyed to them the truth of God. But suddenly he was gone, creating a vacuum of leadership.

In this situation the disciples were paralyzed. They did not have the necessary guidance to undertake new initiatives, deal with new questions and problems, or set out in new directions. All they could do was follow the last instructions Jesus had given them. They could remain in Jerusalem until the promise Jesus had talked about was fulfilled. Of course, according to Acts, they did engage in some activities. They prayed (Acts 1:14), something they had done all their lives. Also, they were familiar with the Old Testament from their synagogue training. Heeding what he thought was the ultimate intention of an Old Testament passage, and indicating the new way in which the Old Testament was being understood, Peter led the disciples to fill the place in the Twelve vacated by Judas in his apostasy (Acts 1:16ff.). Today, we would not employ their method of determining the will of God to select a leader. They cast lots after prayer with the expectation that God would control the process so that the one on whom the lot fell would be God's choice. They had Old Testament precedents for this method (Lev 16:8, etc.).[5] However, the disciples' major role—to be witnesses to Jesus' death and resurrection—was totally new. In relation to this role, they were essentially unable to act. They needed directions from the Lord in order to do that, and he was no longer with them.

THE GIFT OF THE SPIRIT

Jesus' physical absence set the stage for the event that took place on Pentecost. One may wonder why the promise affirmed by Jesus was fulfilled on the day of Pentecost. The Greek verb translated "had come" (Acts 2:1) also means "completely filled." It implies that God specifically chose the day on which to fulfill the promise to send the Spirit. Whatever the case, Pentecost was an exceedingly appropriate day for the launching of the missionary effort that was to reach the ends of the earth. Pentecost was one of the three great pilgrim festivals of Judaism. It was a harvest festival, the day when the first fruits of the wheat harvest were presented to the Lord.[6] On that day thousands of Jews from all over the Roman Empire were present for the celebration of the festival in Jerusalem. Although the pilgrims were Jews of the dispersion,[7] they symbolized the far reaches of the world that the good news was meant to penetrate.

In Acts 2:1 we are told "they were all together in one place." Who does "they all" include? In terms of strict grammatical rules, it would refer to the nearest antecedent, that is, to the Twelve mentioned in Acts 1:26. However, it could and probably does refer to the congregation assembled in Jerusalem, "about one hundred twenty persons" (Acts 1:15).[8] Since the community included females along with males, this would indicate that the Spirit was gender neutral, falling on all members of the community alike irrespective of gender. A sound "like the rush of a mighty wind" was the first indication to the assembled disciples that Jesus' word was about to be fulfilled. This was followed by a visual phenomenon, "tongues as of fire," given to each of them. One can hardly miss the symbolism of the two phenomena. Both wind and fire represent the Spirit, and they are used here to affirm that there was no way to mistake what was happening. God's promise was being fulfilled; the disciples were baptized with the Spirit. The immediate result was that they all began to speak in other tongues.[9]

Apparently, what Luke describes in Acts is a miracle either of speaking or hearing. The disciples, who were not among the educated elite, spoke the languages of the Roman world. Attention has often been called to the idea that Pentecost reversed Babel, a symbol of the world's divisions, and represented the bringing together of people from different cultures into one community.

THE MISSION BEGINS

When the Spirit had been given, the mission of the church could begin. From that moment the disciples were no longer leaderless. In the Spirit they had access to the guidance and resources they needed to fulfill the responsibility Jesus gave them. Attracted by the commotion, a crowd gathered. Peter, the usual spokesman for the disciples, stood to explain the event (Acts 2:14ff.). Contrary to what some supposed, the disciples were not drunk. The early hour indicated that. Instead, God had fulfilled what God promised long ago. What the Jewish people had been waiting for had come to pass. The text was from Joel 2:28ff. God poured out his Spirit "on all flesh," that is, on all God's children—sons and daughters, young and old, slave and free.

In the Hebrew Bible, the Spirit of God is quintessentially expressed in the prophetic gift. Here, there, and yonder, according to the Old Testament, God's Spirit had been given to an individual, male or female, in a special way and that individual had become the spokesperson for the message God wanted delivered to their contemporary generation. A common belief among Jews of the first century held that no person had received the gift of prophecy since the time of the last prophet of the Old Testament. For centuries, God had not spoken directly to the people of God, but at the end-time, when the messianic age dawned, that would no longer be true. God's Spirit would be poured out on the people, the gift of prophecy would be one of the results, and God would speak directly to the redeemed community again.

Under the "new covenant" (Jer 31:31), the main difference would be that the Spirit would be given to everybody, not to just a few. All God's children would be endowed with the Spirit. The result would be that both their sons and their daughters would prophesy (Joel 2:28), i.e., proclaim the message of God for their contemporaries. Thus, on Pentecost the community of the Spirit came into being. No longer would the prophetic gift be a possibility for the very few. All believers, male and female, possessed the Spirit of prophecy. Any member of the congregation could deliver God's contemporary message to the church.

No better text exists than the one Peter used in that first sermon to demonstrate that women and men are both given the gifts essential to preaching. Females are prophets in both the Old and New Testaments.[10] The essential difference now is that every believing woman, not just one here and there, becomes a possible recipient of the message God wants delivered to the people. The prophetic gift, the greatest of all the gifts available to Christians in every age, is the one most indicative of the Spirit's presence.[11]

Suffice it to say, what we were prepared for by Acts 1:8 had begun. With the pouring out of the Spirit, the disciples were able to initiate their witness. Peter preached a sermon in which he described how the God who acted in the history of the people acted in a climactic way by raising Jesus from the dead. This risen Jesus was none other than the Lord and Messiah of Israel!

THE SIGNIFICANCE OF PENTECOST

What is the real significance of Pentecost? The answer is clear. The Lord who had departed from the disciples had returned to be with them in the person of the Spirit. As John 14:18 phrases the promise of Jesus, he had told his disciples," I will not leave you orphaned; I am coming to you." From the moment his followers received the Spirit, they had the guidance they needed. The church would begin to face many questions the disciples had never confronted during the ministry of Jesus and for which there was no specific guidance from his teachings. It would wrestle with new problems, plan for new ministries, and make decisions never faced before.

After Pentecost, however, the church was not helpless in those circumstances. The Spirit of the Lord was present and available to God's people. Through the prophetic gift, which may be given at any moment to any believer, the people would hear God's message of the hour. In a word, the church was no longer handicapped by the lack of Jesus' own presence in its midst. The book of Acts, as do the other books of the New Testament, witnesses to this truth. As the church needed direction, the Lord of the church acting through his Spirit would give it to them through some prophetic voice for that particular moment. The church could solve new problems, answer new questions, and take new initiatives because of the presence of the Spirit.

AUTHORITY AND THE SPIRIT

The gift of the Spirit to the church also meant that there were two foci of authority for the Christian community. The central and decisive focus was the incarnation—the life and teachings of Jesus. Prior to the resurrection, the disciples along with other Jews of the first century believed in the Law as the ultimate expression of the will of God, immutable and eternal. It was the key to interpreting God's revelation in any age. One of the criteria used by the rabbis for including any writing outside the Pentateuch in their authoritative Scripture was coherence with the law. Any work not proven compatible with the Law was ruled out.[12] As we have seen, the disciples took a radically new approach to the interpretation of the Old Testament. The Law was no longer regarded as the crucial, ultimate, and decisive word of God to the people. The resurrection changed everything. After the disciples became convinced that Jesus was alive, they were convinced that God had spoken the ultimate word in Jesus of Nazareth.

From the beginning, the Jewish Scriptures have been a problem to the Christian community. Stories like those in which God gives instructions to eradicate entire peoples are a case in point (Num 31:13ff.; Deut 2:30-35; 20:16-17; and especially 1 Sam 15:1-3). Today we call this ethnic cleansing, an atrocity that we universally condemn.

Early in Christian history two extremes emerged with reference to the Old Testament. A group we generally label as gnostics became a real threat in their understanding of God's revelation. They rejected the Old Testament altogether, claiming that the God of the Jewish Scriptures was not the one Jesus had revealed in his life and ministry.[13] The other extreme, whom we often call Judaizers or legalists, held to a literal interpretation of the Old Testament. According to their view, Christians were obligated to observe all the commandments of the Old Testament. In the second century this position was advanced by a group we call Ebionites.

Fortunately, the major current of Christianity, generally speaking, found its way between the two extremes. The earliest Christians did not abandon the Hebrew Bible but remained firm in the conviction that the God of Abraham, Isaac, Jacob, and the prophets was the God Jesus called "Father." For them the key to interpreting the Old Testament was the revelation of God in Jesus Christ. He was God's ultimate word. He was the center of God's redemptive activity. Starting with the conviction that the risen Christ was the Messiah of Jewish expectation, they began to understand the Old Testament in a radically different way. They saw it as a prelude to the main act of salvation history and not the main act itself. They began to read the Old Testament books looking for those passages that were coherent with what God had done in Christ. From the New Testament writings we see that Jesus took a liberal approach to understanding the Law. As we have seen in an earlier chapter, he did not hesitate to set aside certain laws that he believed were not in keeping with the two central commandments of God. A superficial examination of their writings will suffice to show that neither Paul in the major epistles nor the writer of Hebrews could be called biblical literalists.

THE AUTHORITY OF THE SPIRIT

As stated above, however, the teaching and life of Jesus often did not give answers to the question of what the Lord of the church wanted his church to do in this new circumstance. This was especially true as the church moved out of the Jewish world into the Gentile world where it faced a totally different set of beliefs, morals, customs, etc. Clear examples are the question of food offered to idols, the matter of marriage with pagans, and other issues treated by Paul in 1 Corinthians. This was no handicap, though, because the community possessed the Spirit, which was the second focus of authority for the earliest Christians. In much of the New Testament we witness theology in its most formative stage as answers were given to new questions and solutions were sought to new problems.

However, a grave danger lurked. Anybody could claim for herself or himself the gift of prophecy and declare that the Lord had revealed a new truth in a vision or in some other way. The history of Christianity is replete with such claims. It is also filled with examples of how easily people can be captivated by a charismatic leader who claims to have special spiritual powers and knowledge of God. The first epistle of John gives a prime example of this phenomenon in the New Testament. Apparently charismatic leaders made gnostic-like statements that were accepted by at least some of the Christians addressed in the epistle. From the gnostic perspective, God, who was good, was pure Spirit and had nothing to do with matter, which was intrinsically evil. The divine Christ, therefore, the bearer of God's revelation to humankind, could not have been a real man and could not have really died on the cross. Gnostics explained the crucifixion in various ways, but all of them were designed to show that the Christ had not suffered and died. In gnostic thought, Jesus was primarily revealer and not redeemer. Salvation came through esoteric and heavenly knowledge, the knowledge they were privy to as a result of their prophetic gift.

First John was written in a pastoral effort to help the churches in the crisis created by these prophets. The epistle teaches that the truth cannot be known apart from God's revelation in the ministry, death, and resurrection of Jesus. Contrary to the false teaching, Jesus was a real man who really died. The truth was what they had heard from the beginning, that is, the witness to Jesus (1 John 1:1-4). From him and as a result of what he had done they learned that God was creating a community of people who love each other. They also needed to recognize that only those who loved the other members of their Christian family approached the reality embodied in and taught by Jesus (1 John 4:7-8). The believers needed to understand that whatever God did in the past and whatever God would do through his Spirit in the future had to be coherent with the revelation in Jesus Christ. This is the only way to approach God's truth revealed by the Spirit.

Salvation by knowledge created divisions in the churches. In direct contrast, salvation through faith in Jesus as gracious redeemer created unity. The refusal to believe that Christ had died on the cross undercut the major revelation of God to humankind, that is, that all people are objects of a love without measure (1 John 4:10). It removed the foundation for the creation of community. The writer of 1 John, therefore, proceeded from the assumption that the Spirit does not undercut what Jesus was and did. Anyone who denied the reality of Jesus' humanity was a false prophet; the spirit that inspired him or her was not of God (1 John 4:1-2). The Spirit's actions had to be coherent with Jesus' words and deeds. Therefore, the message, which brought about love for God's family, was the only one that could come from God. John, as did Paul, identified the Spirit primarily with love—with love expressed concretely in community (cf. Rom 5:5).

PROBLEMS

Early on, the church was put on the defensive as it confronted teachings brought about by a distorted gnostic emphasis on the authority of the Spirit. One of the results was that the bishop was given more and more authority in the region under his influence to define what was doctrinally accepted. This developed into the doctrine that the teaching authority belonged to the church represented by its bishops and that the Bible was not subject to individual interpretation. As doctrinal disputes arose in the early centuries, the issues were generally resolved through a conference of bishops (called a synod) that defined orthodoxy for the churches. Thus, a certain uniformity of belief could be secured in large regions of the world. Of course, this was a position challenged by the Reformers. All people, equipped as believers with the leadership of the Spirit, have the capacity and responsibility to grasp for themselves what God wants them to know.

Admittedly, there is no real control for those of us who reject the belief that there is no exterior authority beyond the individual believer. Many people, all disagreeing with one another, claim to know what God's truth really is. The chaos the Roman Catholic Church feared and took steps to contain soon became a reality in Protestantism, which is represented by innumerable diverse groups in the world, each one claiming that theirs is the only true approach to faith and practice. In modern times, television exacerbates this situation. In spite of the apparent problems, however, those of us in the Protestant tradition do not want to surrender our right to interpret Scripture for ourselves to a group of people whom we believe to be as fallible as we are.[14]

Modern fundamentalism reacts to Christian diversity in a way that repeats early history. Assuming that they know the mind of God, the group that is in power defines orthodoxy, and that definition becomes a creed, although it may be called a confession of faith. All members of that group are then forced to accept the creed in order to remain a part of the group, and in this way uniformity is achieved. One may see this process occurring in several mainline denominations.

In my opinion, this problem of divisions among Christian groups can only be resolved by adopting two approaches. In the first place, we need to approach the Bible with humility, recognizing that all of us are fallible and that all our theology is faulty. As Paul declared in 1 Corinthians 13:12, all our knowledge is partial. Second, we need to put the emphasis where the writer of 1 John put it. We need to be able to transcend our differing conclusions about beliefs and practices with the recognition that all people who trust the God whom we have come to know through the revelation in Jesus are our brothers and sisters. The major truth of the New Testament is that God is creating a community of people who love one another. If we are unorthodox in that, we are wrong in what is most important. No community as wide as God's church is possible if we require that all people say their theology exactly as we do.

A division also exists between people over the question of the relationship of Scripture and Spirit. Some people today teach that everything the church needs to be the church in the world today is found in the Bible. They affirm confidently that everything they do is patterned after the churches in the New Testament. As we noted in an earlier chapter, it is impossible to pattern church structure by the New Testament because we know so little about church life in the earliest days. Such a position leads to a wooden and unimaginative approach to being the people of God in the contemporary world. It is also guilty of the failure to understand that God still speaks to people today. The word of God spoken to the community of believers today is as much the word of God as anything said two thousand years ago. The ministry of the prophet continues to be as essential as it was in the early years.[15]

On the other hand, some people place too much weight on the latest vision, the latest revelation, their "experience" of the Spirit. They do not, as 1 John 4:1 teaches us to do, put the spirits to the test of coherence with God's revelation in Jesus. Often the resulting expressions of Christianity are extremely eccentric. Both of the approaches described above can promote arrogance and division in the body of Christ, exactly the opposite of the work of the Spirit, the source (according to Eph 4:3) of the unity of the church. When Jesus is truly Lord of his church, his Spirit leads the people to love one another. Surely this is one of the clearest aspects of New Testament teaching about the Lord's will for the people of God.

THE SIGNIFICANCE OF PENTECOST FOR NEW BELIEVERS

We must address another question raised for modern believers by the account of Pentecost. What relation does the experience of the earliest Christians have to our receiving the gift of the Spirit? This question is raised because some groups teach that modern Christians must recapitulate the experience of the earliest disciples, basing their belief on their interpretation of Acts. According to the interpretation of these people, often called pentecostals or charismatics, the water baptism of the disciples did not bring them into the fullness of the believer's experience. They also needed the additional baptism of the Spirit, which they received on the day of Pentecost. In the same way, these groups contend, confession of faith in Jesus and water baptism are also inadequate for modern believers. It is essential for them to be baptized with the Spirit. Water baptism and Spirit baptism can both occur at the same time. In actual practice, however, the two often take place at different times. Sometimes it is years after one professes faith in Christ and is baptized that the individual senses a need for something more, a greater filling with the Spirit. According to some Christians, this need is satisfied when the individual has been baptized with the Spirit. People often testify that only after they were baptized with the Spirit did they at last have spiritual power, joy, and peace. The tendency of such groups is to create two classes of Christians—those who have received the baptism of the Spirit and those who have only received water baptism.

Various problems arise in connection with this interpretation. First, it fails to take into account the uniqueness of the apostolic pilgrimage. It assumes that every Christian has to recapitulate the experience of the earliest followers of Jesus. However, it is obvious that the road to faith walked by the earliest disciples was different from that taken by any believers since that time. Evidently some of the followers of Jesus were first followers of John the Baptist and were baptized by him in Jordan. Then they were attracted to Jesus and followed him. Only that generation of disciples could witness his death. Only to that generation did Jesus give such vivid assurances through his post-resurrection appearances that God had raised him from the dead. Only that generation received the Spirit subsequent to their relationship with the earthly Jesus.

Since that time, all Christians have lived on this side of John the Baptist, on this side of the incarnation, on this side of the crucifixion, on this side of the resurrection, and on this side of the moment when the church received the Spirit. Faith in Jesus Christ as the Risen One, inclusion with the company of the earliest disciples in the Christian community, and the possibility of growing in that fellowship are all achievable only through the ministry of the Spirit.

THE TESTIMONY OF THE NEW TESTAMENT

The New Testament uniformly takes the position that conversion itself is only possible through the Spirit. From the moment of conversion, every Christian is assumed to have the Spirit. A few examples will serve to make the point. One of Paul's words for Christians is "saints," a word that implies they have the Spirit. This is a name given to the Corinthian Christians (1 Cor 1:2). And he associates with them "all those who in every place call on the name of our Lord Jesus Christ." This says that calling on the name of Jesus, i.e., Christian prayer, is evidence that the people are saints or "sanctified ones." In verse 7 of the same chapter the apostle also thanks God that the Corinthian recipients "are not lacking in any spiritual gift," something impossible apart from the Spirit. Yet anyone who reads the letter knows that the church was about as imperfect as a church can be. Obviously most, if not all, of them were not acquainted with the "abundant life," which some Christians affirm to be the result of baptism with the Spirit.

Who has the Spirit? How does the Spirit express itself in an individual's life? What is the relation of the Spirit to the gifts the Christian receives? Does a spectacular gift mean that one individual is more spiritual than another? Questions like these seem to lie behind what Paul writes in 1 Corinthians 12–14. One of the first points he made in his treatment of this question is found in 1 Corinthians 12:1-3. Paul does not want the believers in Corinth to be confused by their pagan background. The verbs used by Paul in 12:2 can refer to being caught up and swept along in an ecstatic experience.

The people of Greece were acquainted with the worship of Dionysius, the god of wine and ecstasy, and with the ecstatic experiences that devotees of that cult had. Christians also could experience ecstasy, seen in such manifestations as speaking in tongues in Corinth. However, just because people became emotional and spoke in tongues did not mean that they possessed the Spirit of God. In fact, such ecstatic experiences did not really distinguish them from the pagans among whom they lived. Paul wanted the Corinthian believers to understand that *the form of an experience is not a guarantee of its validity*. Rather, the presence of the Spirit is best seen in the simple and public declaration, "Jesus is Lord" (1 Cor 12:3). It is generally agreed that this confession is the primitive Gentile baptismal confession of faith. It was the first indication that a person was converted and possessed the Spirit. It is impossible to make the kind of confession one makes in a public profession of faith without the ministry of the Spirit. Or, as Paul states the idea, no person can say, "Jesus is Lord," except by the Holy Spirit.

From this we can only conclude that every Christian has the Spirit from the very first moment of faith. In another place Paul affirms that the person who does not have the Spirit does not belong to Christ (Rom 8:9).[16] Paul joins the writer of 1 John in arguing that the primary expression of the Spirit's presence is the love the people have for one another. Therefore, 1 Corinthians 13 is essential to Paul's argument about the Spirit in chapters 12 and 14. In this connection we remember Luke's report that Jesus selected a text from Isaiah to read in the synagogue service, a text that describes the effect of the Spirit on his life and ministry: "The Spirit of the Lord is upon me, because he has anointed me to bring good news to the poor. He has sent me to proclaim release to the captives and recovery of sight to the blind, to let the oppressed go free, to proclaim the year of the Lord's favor"

(Luke 4:18). In other words, the Spirit's presence in Jesus' life is seen in a ministry of compassion.

In the context of the Pentecostal experience itself, we find the statement given by Peter as an answer to the query of the multitude: "Repent, and be baptized every one of you in the name of Jesus Christ so that your sins may be forgiven; and you will receive the gift of the Holy Spirit" (Acts 2:38). No conditions are set. When a person becomes a child of God and sins are forgiven, God gives the Spirit to that individual. No contingencies are attached in Peter's sermon. In Acts Peter is described as justifying his baptism of Cornelius and his people to the Jewish community. There he clearly associates faith in Jesus with reception of the Spirit when he says, "If then God gave them the same gift that he gave us *when we believed* in the Lord Jesus Christ, who was I that I could hinder God?" (Acts 11:17).[17]

In connection with what has been said above, one might raise the following question: At what moment did the first followers of Jesus become believers? Admittedly no one is able to do what God alone can do. No one can decide exactly at what point any individual receives God's redemptive grace. Nevertheless, if one views the question in the light of the total teaching of the New Testament—that a believer is a person who has received the Spirit of God—then one must answer that the disciples became believers when they received the Spirit. Indeed, according to the Acts account, Peter apparently identified Pentecost as the moment of the apostles' conversion, as we have seen above.

NOTES

[1] With the kind of overweening arrogance of some people who dare to assume they know the mind of God, one minister said, "God does not hear the prayers of Jews." This is hardly the picture one gets from the practice of Jesus and the early disciples who joined their fellow Jews in worship.

[2] The Christian church is considered the community of the last days, the eschatological community in technical language, because it was believed that the last days dawned with the resurrection of Jesus.

[3] See Isa 4:4; 32:15; 44:3; Ezek 11:19; 36:26; Joel 3:1; Zech 12:10.

[4] Joel 2:28; cf. Jer 31:31-34.

[5] Compare this decision with the one described in Acts 13:1-3, when the church had the guidance of the Spirit.

[6] Subsequent to New Testament times, Pentecost became a feast commemorating the giving of the Torah, the Law.

[7] The dispersion or the Diaspora refers to Jews living outside their homeland.

[8] From Paul's account we learn that there were more than 500 believers at this time (1 Cor 15:6).

[9] It is instructive to note that all the assembled members received the Spirit at the same time. This is characteristic of Acts. When we are told that the Spirit came upon a group of people, all received that gift at the same time.

[10] For a fuller discussion, see "Women in the Church."

[11] We shall return to this subject in the discussion of ministry.

[12] The rabbis at Jamnia around AD 90 made the final definition of the Jewish canon using this and other criteria.

[13] Marcion is a major representative of this approach. He rejected the Old Testament and accepted one gospel, commonly regarded as the Gospel according to Luke, along with the Pauline epistles as his New Testament. He purged these of Old Testament references that he regarded as additions to the original text. This is the first known attempt to define a New Testament canon.

[14] Walter Shurden has raised an important question: "Is there any community to which we are accountable?" He also suggested a solution: "Perhaps to the local community." When I was last pastor of a church, I told the people: "I will be subject to the decisions you make if you will listen to my ideas about the issue at stake." I believe that the decision of an informed group will generally be better than that of the individual isolated from the group. Of course, there are moral issues on which I would not want to yield to any individual or group. For example, the matter of race or gender discrimination is not a matter for debate as far as I am concerned.

[15] For more on the prophet, see the chapter on ministry.

[16] See also 1 John 2:23; 4:2f.

[17] My italics. Two passages in Acts tell about the Spirit being given later than the moment of conversion (8:14-17; 19:1-7). However, these are difficult passages that are subject to interpretations bringing them into line with the clear teaching elsewhere in the New Testament. For a fuller discussion of these passages, see *Speaking in Tongues* by Fisher Humphreys and Malcolm Tolbert (New Orleans: Insight Press, 1973).

Baptism: The Door into the Church

We now turn to the question of how one became a member of a church in the New Testament era. Contrary to the practice of many religions in ancient and modern times, in the beginning a person did not become a member of the Christian community by being born into a certain family, tribe, or nation. There was indeed continuity between the Christian church and Judaism, and there was great similarity in the beliefs of Christians and pharisaic Jews. Christianity, however, was something new if we define Christians as followers of Christ.

Prior to the earliest believers that the New Testament describes, there were no people who accepted Jesus as God's Messiah, their redeemer, and the ultimate revelation of God to humankind. In the beginning, the church was formed of people who made individual decisions to follow Christ. The crucial act by which they proclaimed their decision (professed their faith) and established their identity in relation to the church was baptism in water. It is important to note that baptism was also the act by which they decisively severed their relationship with the pagan world.

THE ORIGIN OF BAPTISM

Obviously the beginning of Christian baptism was related to the practice of John the Baptizer who called on people to repent—to turn toward God in anticipation of the imminent and decisive demonstration of God's kingly power (kingdom) for which so many people ostensibly had been longing. He asked all who heeded his message to indicate their decision by presenting themselves to him on the banks of the river Jordan to be baptized. Baptism, therefore, was a crucial act embraced by individual Jews. Through it, they announced that they were ceasing their rebellion against God and turning toward God in openness to the impending future announced by John. One needs to understand that the atmosphere in Palestine was highly charged with the expectation that the coming of the Messiah was at hand; the people heard John's preaching in that context.

We would like to know more about John, but his biography was not important to the Gospel writers or to early Christians. The primary reason for beginning the gospel story with a brief account of John's ministry was the way it fit into the early Christian interpretation of the Hebrew Scriptures. According to the Gospel writers' interpretation of the Old Testament, John's ministry fulfilled the prophecies found in Isaiah and Malachi. He was the voice crying in the wilderness referred to in Isaiah 40:3.[1] John was God's messenger promised in Malachi 3:1, the forerunner who would prepare the way before the Lord. What this meant was that John was the Elijah who, according to Malachi 4:5, would be sent "before the great and terrible day of the LORD [came]." Elijah's appearance meant, therefore, that the Messiah was about to make his entrance into the world.

But why did John ask people to make baptism such a decisive act, marking the radical change in their lives? We recognize immediately that water, with its cleansing and purifying properties, lends itself to many obvious uses in religious symbolism. Thus, it is not surprising that John used it to signify cleansing from sin. More than that, it may be significant that the Essene headquarters, the Qumran community, was located near the place where John preached and baptized. That community, which was dedicated to preparing the way of the Lord in the wilderness (see note 1) through its ritual purity and strict observance of the Law, had a baptismal pool and engaged in numerous washings for purification. According to one hypothesis, John adopted his practice from them. Some have even suggested that John may have been reared in that community (see Luke 1:80).

Another possibility is that baptism was suggested to John by the ritual required of proselytes. Converts to Judaism may have been requested to submit to baptism as a part of their ritual of acceptance into the Jewish community. We know that this was true a few years after John's time, but we have no concrete evidence that it was a Jewish practice contemporary with his ministry. Be that as it may, and for reasons that must remain obscure to us, John decided that baptism was an appropriate way for people to express their decision to repent in anticipation of what God had in store for them.

John's practice must have been somewhat distinctive; otherwise, he would not have been called "the Baptizer." His actions differed in important ways from the first-century baptisms about which we know. Jewish proselyte baptism was for Gentiles who converted to Judaism. John, however, was calling on Jews to repent and be baptized. Also, in contrast to Essene practice, John's baptism was evidently a one-time event and did not involve repeated washings.

JESUS' BAPTISM

The baptism of Jesus by John served as a crucial link between John's practice and the adoption of baptism by the Christian community. Nevertheless, it evidently created a problem for early believers. How could they account for the fact that Jesus was baptized by a person inferior to him? It is even possible that members of a John the Baptist sect used this to assert their superiority over the followers of Jesus.[2] All four Gospels deal with this issue, which indicates how much of a problem it was for the earliest disciples (Matt 3:11ff.; Mark 1:7; Luke 3:15-17; John 1:19-35). These writings make it clear that John rejected the idea that he was the Messiah and recognized and announced the superiority of Jesus.

Another often-discussed problem arises in connection with Jesus' baptism. John was calling sinners to repentance, to a baptism by which people announced the radical change that had occurred in their lives. Did this mean that Jesus also saw himself as a sinner, a notion consistently rejected by classical orthodoxy? According to Matthew 3:15, when John hesitated to baptize him, Jesus' response to his objection was "Let it be so now; for it is proper for us to fulfill all righteousness." Too often we define righteousness in a negative sense as the absence of sin. However, there is a positive and more important aspect of this quality. Righteousness describes a life lived in faithfulness to God. Rather than an admission of sin, therefore, Jesus' baptism can be interpreted as a public declaration of his commitment to God's will for his life.

In a sense, Jesus' baptism was the moment of his ordination to be God's Messiah. At that moment the heavenly voice declared: "This is my Son, the Beloved, with whom I am well pleased" (Matt 3:17), an allusion to Psalm 2:7, an enthronement psalm. To Jewish Christians, this meant that Jesus was the long-awaited King Messiah, the descendant of David. In his baptism Jesus not only committed himself to a messianic ministry, but from later Gospel texts (for example, Mark

8:31 and parallels), we learn that Jesus understood his ministry to be one of a suffering Messiah, a concept totally foreign to contemporary Jewish expectations. Later, Jesus also referred to his anticipated suffering as his baptism, thus linking the end with the beginning of his ministry (Mark 10:38). Through his baptism, Jesus also declared that he identified with the remnant God was gathering through John, the redeemed remnant of the end time.

We conclude, therefore, that Christian baptism originated in John's practice, was undergirded by the baptism of Jesus at the beginning of his ministry, and was adopted from the beginning as the moment when one became a member of the community God was bringing into being—the moment when one was included in the fellowship of the redeemed.

THE FORM OF BAPTISM

It seems to me that in a discussion of baptism in the New Testament one must make a clear distinction between the form of baptism and its meaning. By so doing, we can lay a foundation for our own approach to baptism, especially with reference to other members of the Christian community whose form may differ from the one we adopt.

There is no need for an extensive discussion of the form of baptism in the New Testament. Almost without doubt, it was immersion, the most common meaning of the Greek word group. The verb *baptizein*[3] is used in various senses, but it most likely denotes "to immerse," "to dip in water." The translators of the Authorized Version (King James) avoided the issue of defining it by transliterating the Greek terms instead of translating them. In this way the English word group—baptist, baptize, baptism—came into being. John baptized in the Jordan River, which strengthens the conclusion that he baptized by immersion. The description of the event also says that Jesus came up out of the water (Mark 1:10).

Furthermore, various passages in the New Testament seem to require the understanding that baptism was by immersion.[4] A good example is in the striking passage, Romans 6:1ff., where Paul states: "Therefore we have been buried with him by baptism into death." The comment by the Catholic scholar Joseph A. Fitzmeyer, S. J., on this passage is fairly typical: "The baptismal rite symbolically represents the death, burial, and resurrection of Christ; the convert descends into the baptismal bath, is covered in its waters, and emerges to a new life."[5] In other words, the act lying behind the symbolism of the passage is baptism by immersion.

Early on, however, there are indications that the form of baptism was not considered immutable. The Didache was a Christian manual written in the early part of the second century to instruct churches. This document gives the following direction: Churches were to baptize in running water. If there was no running water, they were to baptize in cold water. If there was no cold water, they could baptize in warm. If this were impossible, they were allowed to pour water three times on the head (7:13). We can see that the exigencies of a dry area could make baptism in a river or in a tank practically impossible. However, wooden adherence to a certain form was not to prevent the convert from being becoming integrated into the community.

THE MEANING OF BAPTISM

We turn now to a discussion of the meaning of baptism. Ideas about this vary widely. On the one extreme, there is the view that God imparts redemptive grace through baptism, quite apart from any decision made by the person who is baptized. God does efficacious work through baptism even though the person being baptized is unconscious or is a newly born infant. On the other extreme is the view of radical Protestants, including Baptists. In such an environment we often hear baptism described as a symbol—sometimes "just a symbol."

A study of the New Testament passages seems to lead to the conclusion that both these extremes are open to question. If baptism is just a symbol, as some insist, it goes without saying that nothing really happens to the individual at the moment of experiencing baptism. It is true that baptism is symbolic. The person being baptized gives a witness and presents the gospel in picture—the picture of the death, burial, and resurrection of Jesus, as well as a picture of the spiritual experience of the baptized. Nevertheless, if baptism is only a symbol, what is really important has already happened. The person has already trusted in Christ, and God has already performed the work of grace in the person's life. This interpretation, however, seems to do an injustice to certain passages, like Romans 6:1-4 and Colossians 2:12, which make the moment of burial with Christ and the beginning of the life of faith contemporaneous with the act of baptism.

Rather than being a symbol of something that God had already done in the life of the new believer, baptism in the New Testament seems to have been the moment when personal faith was confessed publicly and saving grace was received. Presenting oneself for baptism apparently was the way a person made the decision and the vehicle through which he or she expressed it. Luke describes the people in John the Baptizer's audience as "the crowds that came out to be baptized by him" (3:7). In other words, they presented themselves to be baptized as an expression of their repentance. Baptism was the decisive moment of turning from sin and turning toward God. It was the moment in which people acted to identify themselves and declare their intention. It was also the moment in which God acted by making them a part of the people he was creating. In this way, God through John was preparing a people for the coming of the expected Messiah.

In his letter to the Galatians, Paul makes this statement: "As many of you as were baptized into Christ have clothed yourselves with Christ" (3:27). This statement implies several things. The only believers Paul knew had been baptized. The way he knew they were believers was through the public act of baptism. The moment of baptism and the moment of conversion, therefore, were the same. In other words, people turned to Christ by presenting themselves to be baptized. Baptism marked the beginning of the convert's new life as a follower of Christ and a member of his redeemed community.

EVANGELICAL PRACTICES IN AMERICA

Evangelicals face a problem in their attempt to rediscover the meaning of baptism for people in the earliest times. In American evangelicalism, the public profession of faith has been distinguished from baptism, often separated from it by a considerable expanse of time. Thus, a person may make a public profession of faith to an individual or in a mass meeting, such as a Billy Graham revival, that has no connection with a church. In many cases, the person who makes a profession of faith is never baptized and may never become a member of a church. This practice probably began in the revival movements that swept America in colonial and later times. We know that earlier and elsewhere we never encounter evidence that the profession of faith is separated from baptism.

In Baptist churches in the South, people typically are asked to come to the front of the congregation as a sign that they are professing their faith in Christ. When people respond in this way, we conclude immediately that the individual, if not already Christian, has at that moment made a decision to follow Christ. Jokingly I have told my classes that five hundred years from now people could conclude that we believed and taught that individuals became Christians by walking down the aisle of a church building.

In certain circles, making a profession of faith is often referred to as "walking the aisle for Jesus." I have often heard my students say, "Two people walked the aisle in our church Sunday." This would be foreign language to the uninitiated, but to those of us who grew up in such circles the meaning is clear. Two people made public professions of faith. It is true that prior to this public profession of faith, the individuals may have expressed their determination to do so in a conversation with the pastor or another person. In evangelical circles the moment of belief in Jesus is the moment of salvation. However, the moment of belief can also be the moment the person walks to the front of the church. An evangelistic appeal is often phrased thus: "If you are not a Christian but believe God is speaking to you, all you have to do is to walk down here and profess Christ publicly." In such instances people can and do believe that walking down the aisle of the church is in itself the decisive moment—when the person expresses a decision arrived at in that moment to trust Jesus as Savior. In the same way, many people may well conclude from the New Testament references that early Christians were redeemed through baptism.

When the moment of faith is the moment when a person goes to the front of the church to make a public profession, walking down the aisle is not symbolic; it is the moment of salvation, recognized as such by the congregation. If that is true, it is also the moment when God acts to redeem—a sacramental moment, if you will. When one understands it in this way, baptism in the New Testament is both a symbol and a sacrament. We can express decisions by words, but we can also do so by actions that are understood by people in our circles in a certain way. Actions, such as walking down a church aisle or presenting oneself for baptism, convey messages just as words do, often more impressively.

BAPTISM AS THE PUBLIC PROFESSION OF FAITH

In contrast to the practice of many contemporary evangelicals, we have already noted that in the earliest churches, baptism appears to have been the decisive moment in which a person became a Christian or, at the very least, was recognized by others as a Christian. It seems probable also that at the time of baptism the individual made a verbal confession of faith. New Testament scholars have identified passages in the New Testament that they believe contain the verbal confession made by people being baptized. Such a passage is found in Romans 10:9: ". . . because if you confess with your lips, 'Jesus is Lord,' and believe in your heart that God raised him from the dead, you will be saved."[6] In the text, Paul does not make a distinction between believing and confessing. They are two sides of the same reality.[7] For Paul, genuine belief was expressed in confession. If our perception is sound, baptism furnished the occasion for this initial confession of faith.

Another relevant text is 1 Corinthians 12:3. In this context, Paul argues that it is dangerous to use ecstasy as proof of the presence of God's Spirit.[8] Rather, the first evidence of the presence of the Spirit in an individual's life is the intelligible confession of faith. "Jesus is Lord" was the primitive Gentile confession of faith probably made for the first time at baptism. This text shows that Paul connected the gift of the Spirit to the act of believing and confessing.

The Western text of Acts,[9] which some scholars hold to be superior to other text types preferred by translators, may help us see the point here. In 8:36 the eunuch, upon seeing water, asked Philip, "What is to prevent me from being baptized?" In 8:37 the Western text contains an answer to the question, omitted by most modern translations. In it Philip replies, "If you believe with all your heart, you may." The eunuch responds, "I believe that Jesus Christ is the Son of God." Following this, both went down into the water, and Philip baptized the eunuch (Acts 8:38). Thus, profession of faith is closely connected to baptism.

BAPTISM AS A DEFINING MOMENT

It is difficult for Christians in the United States to understand what a decisive event baptism was for the earliest Christians. In the modern environment, nothing may actually change outwardly for us if we decide to become members of a church. We will not be persecuted because of it. We do not have to fear going to prison or losing our jobs. Rather than constituting a political liability, being a member of a church in the United States is generally viewed as an asset. That was not the case, of course, in early Christianity. To become a Christian could very well mean that a believer would suffer ostracism, persecution, and even the loss of life.

In such a situation baptism was the defining moment. Prior to presenting themselves to be baptized, people had nothing to fear. Before baptism, they were still identified with the pagan or Jewish world. When they were baptized, however, they crossed the divide. Their baptism was the public act by which they became identified with the Christian church, a despised minority. In that situation, baptism was certainly more than "just a symbol." It was a moment of tremendous personal import, and being baptized was in and of itself a wrenching and life-changing event. It was also the moment in which people experienced the redemptive grace of God.

People who have pursued their ministry in lands hostile to Christianity, or at least to their kind of Christianity, know the truth of what I am saying. They know that the decisive moment is not when a person confides in them the desire to become a Christian; rather, it is the public act of baptism. Baptism is the way in which converts identify themselves clearly with reference to Christ and a despised Christian group, often with serious consequences, i.e., the loss of family, job, even life. All of us have heard missionaries tell the stories about secret Christians who do not have the courage to become members of the church because of their fear of the consequences. The act of baptism is much more demanding and difficult than a private confession of personal faith. Certain circumstances, similar to the ones believers faced in the first century, demand a greater amount of courage and commitment and are therefore more meaningful.

SACRAMENT OR ORDINANCE

Words such as sacrament and ordinance are post-New Testament terms that identify differing theological positions. Sacrament emphasizes the activity of God in an event. Ordinance distinguishes the act as one that conforms to the instruction given by Jesus. By express command and example the New Testament shows us that the practice of baptism is very important. If the discussion above has merit, however, baptism as practiced in New Testament churches was far more than an act of obedience. It was an event that radically changed the direction of an individual's life. This was true for John's baptism and for Christian baptism. As a decisive moment, it was also a moment in which God's redemptive grace was imparted—one in which a relationship between God and the individual came into being and in which a person was included in God's family, the church.

Consider this illustration. Imagine that you have been taken captive with a group of other church members, and the moment has come for you to face a firing squad to be executed for your faith along with others. However, you are given one last opportunity to avoid death. The commander of the firing squad says, "All of you who insist on confessing Christ as Lord, step forward to be executed." Under those circumstances, would the confession made by stepping forward be *just a symbol*? The answer is obvious. It would be the expression of the most fateful decision you ever made. Would it not also be a sacramental moment? After all, in order to make such a decision you would need the presence and power of God as never before. Through the centuries, when they stepped forward to be baptized, many Christians have lived out this illustration, thus placing life and future in jeopardy.

INFANT BAPTISM

Two major points have been made thus far: (1) the most primitive mode of baptism was by immersion, and (2) baptism was the means by which the individual expressed a personal decision to follow Jesus. If we assume that these are correct, it is easy to see that the practice of infant baptism creates certain problems. As we begin our discussion of infant baptism, practiced widely by Christian churches today, let us say up front that the New Testament is silent about the issue. There is no text in the New Testament that explicitly deals with the question of the status of children born into Christian homes. Being born to Christian parents clearly differed from being born in a pagan household, but this is not a subject for discussion in the New Testament texts.[10] True, the baptism of children became a practice very early in the Christian church. It grew more and more important as the years passed. To a great extent, this was in connection with the evolving theology about original sin and the efficacy of baptism to cleanse infants who were thought to have "been born in sin."

Many denominations have rejected this extreme sacramental understanding of baptism but have continued the practice of infant baptism. They have simply redefined its meaning. Through it they recognize that children born to believers are also included in the household of faith. It also gives the church an opportunity to affirm her responsibility as a Christian family. Furthermore, parents can commit themselves to rearing their children in a Christian environment. Usually such churches also make provision for the children to make their own decision of faith at the time of confirmation.

In support of the practice of infant baptism, the texts most often referred to are found in Acts, especially in the accounts of the conversion and baptism of Lydia (Acts 16:14-15) and the Philippian jailer (Acts 16:30-33). In the first account we read that Lydia "and her household" were baptized. In the second we are told that the family of the jailer was baptized. In common usage the "household" included children as well as other members of the family, servants, and slaves. These leave open the possibility that infants may have been included among those who were baptized. This argument, however, is an argument from silence, which is never considered good evidence in an objective study. There is simply no clear evidence in the New Testament that infant baptism was practiced in any church.

The interpretation discussed above also can be dangerous because it leaves open a possible justification for a practice widely followed in later times (the Protestant Reformation, for example) when the decision of the ruler was considered valid for all the citizens under his domain. Do the texts in Acts mean that other, more mature members of the household were taken into the church without exercising personal faith themselves? Was Lydia's decision determinative for everyone else? Or was this a way of indicating that members of Lydia's household were also reached by the gospel? We simply do not have the evidence for determining an answer to these questions.

What has been said above notwithstanding, the weight of New Testament evidence goes against basing infant baptism on the text of Scripture. What I mean by this is that there is not one instance in the New Testament that furnishes clear evidence that an infant underwent baptism. Furthermore, many texts indicate that the decisive action on the part of the individual was his or her personal decision for God that laid claim to God's redeeming and transforming grace.

THE CHOICE: FORM OR MEANING

Many Christian churches freely accept members from other denominations without question, whatever their form of baptism may have been. That is not the case, however, with many evangelicals among whom are found a majority of Baptist churches in the South. For them the question is not whether the person has been a Christian for many years, known by all and sundry as a person committed to Christ, unashamedly professing her faith. The issue is not even whether the person has been a good Christian, better than many members of the receiving church. Rather, the question is whether the individual has been baptized by immersion subsequent to or in connection with a personal decision to trust Christ. More than that, in most Baptist churches in the South the question is whether a Baptist minister has immersed the individual in a Baptist church. This attitude can be connected historically to the influence of the thesis propounded in *The Trail of Blood.* According to the argument of that small but influential pamphlet, the church established by Jesus was a Baptist church. All other groups that call themselves churches are nothing more than societies. Only people coming from other Baptist churches, therefore, have experienced valid baptism. In my childhood church only people "of like faith and order," that is, members of Baptist churches, were invited to participate in the Lord's Supper.

Of course today many Baptists would not argue that theirs is the only legitimate church. At the same time, they can be adamant in their support of the requirement that Christians from other denominations be immersed before being accepted as members of their church. There are exceptions to the general practice. Some churches accept baptism from other denominations if it has been by immersion following a personal decision. A very small number of them accept members from other denominations whether they have been immersed or not.

A POST-NEW TESTAMENT PROBLEM

This discussion raises an issue I have faced as a person "born and bred in the Baptist briar patch." Let us assume that the conclusions I have drawn about baptism in the New Testament are correct. They are as follows: (1) Immersion was the form of baptism practiced by churches in New Testament times. (2) Baptism was the decisive moment in which individuals crossed the line between their old life and the new life in Christ; that is, it marked the very beginning of the new life in Christ. (3) Baptism was the moment when the individual being baptized made a verbal profession of faith. God was also active in the baptism, baptizing the person with the Spirit and integrating her or him into the community of faith. (4) The best evidence leads us to conclude that the people baptized were old enough to make such a decision; that is, the textual evidence for infant baptism is not persuasive.

Let us now see where this leaves us. People convinced that immersion is the correct form of baptism in the New Testament and that for it to be valid it must be the result of a decision by the individual involved are confronted with a problem that did not exist in New Testament times. They often have to decide between form and meaning in their approach toward receiving Christians from other churches. Remember that in those days no one was known to be a Christian, so far as we can determine, who had not been baptized. As the moment when the individual professed faith, baptism was the beginning of the Christian life. It was the public proclamation of a decision that enabled people to know that an individual had become identified with the Christian community.

With the multiple denominations that exist today, the situation is totally different. Many believers were baptized as infants, and many of the ones with whom we come into contact were baptized by sprinkling. In the course of time they came to a personal decision of faith. They may have made that decision years ago. As we have said, they may have been recognized by everybody, including their Baptist neighbors and other immersionists, as genuinely devout Christians and as brothers and sisters in Christ. For various reasons, often to unify the family, a person in the category described above frequently wants to become a member of a church that practices baptism by immersion but does not want to be immersed. At times they object to it because they feel it would be a betrayal of their own previous, sincere decision of faith and that it would constitute a denigration of the church of which they have been members.

Theologically, whether they recognize it or not, churches confronted by this situation face a conflict between form and meaning. Immersion apparently was the form of baptism practiced in the early days of Christian history, but—and this is extremely important—it did not take place in the middle of the life of faith. Furthermore, people were not immersed solely because they wanted to be members of another church. Therefore, we may immerse people who present themselves for church membership after they have openly confessed their faith for years, but what they experience cannot be baptism in the New Testament sense. Pastors often recognize this and say in the baptismal liturgy, "I baptize you as a reaffirmation of your faith." Or they may substitute the word "immerse" for baptize. However, there is no New Testament text to support this understanding of the significance of baptism. Rather, baptism at that time was the initial confession of faith. It took place at the beginning of the Christian life and not in the middle.

Clearly there is a conflict between form and meaning in such instances. In such a conflict we have to ask, "Which of the two is most important?" It seems to me that there is only one answer to that question. How individuals make known their decision for faith is not nearly as important as the genuineness of that commitment. Therefore, I have contended for a long time that churches should not require the immersion of people who want to transfer their membership from a church that does not adopt the same practice.

One of the basic motives for rejecting infant baptism in the early years of Baptist history was the desire for a regenerate church as opposed to what the first Baptists saw in the state church of England. However, today I would think that few of us would argue that the membership of a Baptist church that insists on immersion is any more regenerate than a Methodist or a Presbyterian church.

In my opinion, the most serious objection to the practice of churches that are restrictive in their membership requirements related to baptism has to do with the reality of the church. On one occasion I asked a group of people in the church to which I belonged, "Do you believe that Methodists, Catholics, Presbyterians, and others who are genuinely committed to Christ have not been accepted by God in the church?" No one of them would admit to believing that. I recognize that there are many religious groups who believe that only people like them are included in God's flock and teach that God has also excluded those who differ. However, I think most Baptists in the South would not go to such extremes. The most serious problem, therefore, is this: a church that is limited only to people baptized by immersion is smaller than God's church.

AN EVANGELICAL HYBRID

The separation of confession and baptism in the theology and practice of many evangelicals has contributed to an understanding of ecclesiology, the doctrine of the church, that is foreign to the New Testament. In the New Testament, humanity is divided into two groups. One group, by far the largest, is the non-Christian world. The people of God, the church, constitute the other group. According to the evidence of the New Testament documents, there were no Christians, recognized as Christians, who did not belong to the church from the moment of their initial decision manifested in baptism.

The modern practice among evangelicals in which profession of faith and baptism are two separate moments in the Christian experience has created a third group—a hybrid group, if you will. A group identified neither with the world nor the church has come into being. Many people have professed faith in Christ but remain outside the church until they are baptized. Some of them are never baptized.

The practice of making a profession of faith separate and apart from baptism apparently is an American development. There is no record of such a practice in Christian history until it began in this country. We do not know exactly when the first person called on people to make a profession of faith without, at the same time, presenting themselves for church membership. It evidently began, however, in the revivals that swept across this land in the early years of its history. Perhaps an evangelist, preaching to a large group of people, called on them to express their decision for Christ by raising their hands or coming forward in the meeting. This developed into the famous "sawdust trail" of Billy Sunday's revival activities and into "walking down the aisle" in evangelical churches.

The separation of profession from baptism has also contributed to another unfortunate conclusion. Many people assume that the church is optional at best or unnecessary at worst. There is a false notion abroad in the land that one can come into a relationship with God through faith in Christ without belonging to Christ's church, the family of God. The creation of the church, however, is God's doing and not our doing. We cannot belong to God without also belonging to God's people. It is true, therefore, that rightly understood there is no salvation outside the church. None of the writers of the New Testament could conceive of the idea that some people were believers who were not also related to the church.

ACTS 2:38

In this context, permit me to say a word about Acts 2:38, which can be used as the central proof text by Christians for their view that baptism is absolutely essential to forgiveness. Based on this text, some Christian groups have concluded that public profession has to be followed immediately by baptism, or forgiveness is not granted. The vast majority of New Testament texts that relate to the subject do not support the idea that baptism is necessary to receive God's forgiveness.[11] Rather, they underline believing as the way of grasping what God has to offer without any mention of baptism at all.[12]

However, if baptism was generally understood by the churches to involve a profession of faith, as we have contended, Acts 2:38 can be understood in much the same way as Romans 10:9, where Paul teaches that believing and confessing are two sides of the same coin. In Acts 2:38 Peter, giving instructions to the people who had been moved by his sermon, emphasized two things. They were to repent, that is, make a radical about-face in the direction of their lives. They were to be baptized, the act through which they decisively turned toward God, confessing their faith in Jesus as the risen Messiah.

NOTES

[1] The ancient manuscripts do not contain the punctuation marks found in modern translations. The punctuation is based on the decision of editors. In Matt 3:3, a colon follows "wilderness" (NRSV). No such punctuation mark is found in Isa 40:3. This represents two understandings of the text. Isaiah called on people to prepare the way of the LORD in or through the wilderness that lay between Babylon and their homeland. This was the way the Qumran community understood the text. Early Christian interpreters, however, understood the passage as it is presented in the Matthean text. John was in the wilderness of Judea, calling on people to repent.

[2] There are reasons to believe that a John the Baptist sect continued to exist after his death. A small Baptist group located in Mesopotamia and known as Mandaeans claims to be the modern heirs of the movement John began.

[3] The intensive of the verb *bapto*.

[4] An exception is found in Luke 11:38 where the verb refers to washing the hands before eating.

[5] "The Letter to the Romans," *The Jerome Bible Commentary*, vol. 2 (Englewood Cliffs NJ: Prentice-Hall, Inc., 1968), 309.

[6] The translation is mine. Quotation marks, as other marks of punctuation, are not in the ancient texts. Editors follow their judgment in inserting them into the text. I think that the direct quotation better serves the understanding of this text.

[7] I do not know what Paul might have said about "secret" faith. Like all of us, he was not equipped to make a decision about God's ultimate evaluation of people. Apparently, he simply assumed that a person who genuinely believed would confess that belief.

[8] As 1 Cor 14 shows, Paul probably had in mind ecstasy expressed in the gift of tongues. Paul's first concern in 1 Cor 12 was to guard against the confusion of Christian ecstasy with pagan ecstasy. To identify tongues or any other ecstatic expression as proof positive of possession by the Spirit meant that pagan ecstasy would have to be so identified.

[9] The Western text is defined by similarities among certain manuscripts that were copied in the western part of the Roman Empire. Although all hand-copied manuscripts differ from one another, some of them indicate by their similarities that they are cousins, so to speak, and share a certain ancestor or ancestors. The Western text type is identified by scholars as one of the earliest text types.

[10] Some interpreters would see 1 Cor 7:12-16 as an exception. In this passage, Paul discusses the validity of the marriage of a Christian to a pagan. In it he argues that such a marriage is legitimate because the pagan is "consecrated through the wife." Also, the children of such a marriage "are holy." The interpretation depends on whether or not Paul is using the terms as he normally does. Generally, when he calls someone holy, it means that person is a believer. In this case, however, Paul apparently is arguing for the legitimacy of the marriage and the legitimacy of the children of such a marriage.

[11] A prime example is the best known verse in the New Testament, John 3:16.

[12] One of the weaknesses of much use of the New Testament is the reliance on a single text instead of recognizing that an important belief or practice has to be undergirded by a number of texts. An egregious example of this is the practice of baptism for the dead based on a text impossible to interpret with any degree of assurance, 1 Cor 15:29.

The Meaning of Church Membership

In Protestant circles in this country, one does not ask if a person is a believer the way evangelicals in other areas do. Normally the question, should it be asked at all, is "Are you a member of a church?" The next question naturally is "Of what church are you a member?" In the deep South there is a good chance that the individual identifies herself or himself as a member of a Baptist church. But what does that really mean? What can we infer from a positive answer to those questions? Are we to understand that the person is necessarily an active member of the church in which he or she claims membership? In a great percentage of the cases that would be a false inference. The truth is that such a statement may not tell us much about the person who makes it. If the church is a Baptist church in the South, some time in the past the individual presented herself before the congregation to make a profession of faith, and upon immersion her name was presumably entered into the roll of the church as a bona fide member. Or it may mean that the individual presented himself at the close of the service, during the "invitation," and requested that his church letter be transferred to that church. On the surface it does not necessarily mean any more than that. The "church member" may never have returned to participate in a single worship service, may never have contributed one dollar to the budget of the church, may be living a life totally contrary to the basic moral principles of Christian living, and, in fact, may reside thousands of miles away from the church in which he or she claims membership. Nevertheless, it is safe to say that the name of the individual is likely still on the church roll, unless the church has not kept good records.

This concept of church has no support in the New Testament. Granted, it is essential for a modern church of any size in our society to maintain a membership roll. Those who have worked in an urban church will testify to the importance of such records. The church with which I am presently associated is fairly large, and I go to the records often to check on addresses, to determine a person's age, to verify how long that person has been a member of the church (important if you are conducting a funeral service), or to read about the family. The problem is that the practice of keeping church rolls has influenced our understanding of ecclesiology so that church membership has come to mean only that one's name is on a church roll.

Arguments from silence are always precarious, but we can say with assurance that churches in the New Testament era did not have anything like a modern church roll. Few believers possessed reading and writing skills. They would not have felt the need for written records to keep up with church membership. No doubt all church members knew each other by name. From what we gather in reading the documents, in their enthusiasm in the earliest days, all church members would be present at each service if at all possible. Never in the New Testament does a reference to believers or church support the definition of a church member as someone whose name happened to be in the church records. Let us ask, therefore, what church membership signifies in the New Testament.

THE BODY OF CHRIST

Many images are used to designate church members in the New Testament. We find such terms as saints, brothers, and believers. Perhaps the most influential image in recent decades is one that we referred to in a previous chapter. People who belong to the church are members of Christ's body. According to the evidence available to us, the apostle Paul was the first person to use the image of the body to depict the relationship of believers to one another. The initial appearance of the metaphor in our literature is in 1 Corinthians 12:12ff. In my opinion, this is the primary passage with which to begin a discussion about the meaning of church membership.

In 1 Corinthians 12–14, Paul responds to questions the Corinthians asked in a letter he had received from them. His response to their questions begins with 1 Corinthians 7:1, where we find this phrase: "Now concerning the matters about which you wrote." Other questions raised by the Corinthians are addressed in 7:25ff., 8:1ff., and 12:1ff. In each case the clue to the fact that Paul was answering a question is the introductory phrase, "Now concerning."

Unfortunately, we do not have the letter from Corinth. One of the great problems in New Testament interpretation is that it is like listening to only one side of a conversation. Consequently, we do not know the exact phrasing of the issue to which Paul responded in chapters 12–14. The Corinthians had asked about the Spirit, about how one identified a gift of the Spirit or a spiritual person. Evidently, at least some members of the church tended to stress uniformity. That is, one gift, apparently the gift of tongues, was essential to prove that a person had truly received the Spirit. Anyone who had not received this one gift apparently was denigrated, looked down upon as an inferior believer, regarded as one who was not "spiritual" (see 12:21). Paul's comments in chapters 12–14 were his attempt to correct this idea.

He stressed first of all (12:3) that every known follower of Jesus possessed the Spirit. The validity of a person's experience was not determined by a single gift. The problem with using an ecstatic experience, like speaking in tongues, as proof positive that one possessed the Spirit was that pagans who worshiped "dumb idols" also had ecstatic experiences (1 Cor 12:2). They were "led astray to idols." As Barrett writes, "led astray . . . suggests moments of ecstasy experienced in heathen religion, when a human being is (or is believed to be) possessed by a supernatural."[1] According to Paul, therefore, an ecstatic experience is not necessarily the evidence of the Spirit's presence. Rather, an intelligent, intelligible affirmation of faith, such as the one found in 1 Corinthians 12:3, was the evidence of the presence of the Spirit.

In the second place, Paul affirmed that a variety of gifts rather than uniformity gave evidence of the Spirit's presence in the church (1 Cor 12:4-11). A spiritual gift was not given primarily to titillate the recipient of the gift but rather to be used for the welfare of the church, or as Paul expressed it, "for the common good" (12:7). In order to fulfill its vocation in the world, the church needs a variety of gifts. The fullness of the church's ministry is determined by the multiplicity of gifts exercised by its members. Furthermore, Paul stated that the gifts given to each member were determined by the Spirit, "who allots to each one individually just as the Spirit chooses" (12:11). That is to say, it is not the recipient's desire for a gift that determines who gets it but the wisdom of the Spirit, who is concerned about the total ministry of the church.

Consequently, individual members are all different with different gifts, but they are also one. This is the apostle's argument, but how was he to drive it home? At that juncture a powerful image came into play. The human body is a graphic illustration of the nature of the church. The body consists of many members, all equipped to perform different functions. Any single member separated from the body is useless. Each contributes to the function of the body only as it does what it is equipped to do in cooperation with all the others. When all members of the body function as they should, the body is whole. The body is handicapped if any one of its members, no matter how insignificant it may appear to be, does not perform its particular and unique function. The same is true of the church. The wholeness of the church depends on the variety of its members and the way they perform their functions as parts of the body.

Of course, Paul's arguments have great relevance today with reference to modern "charismatics" who claim that baptism of the Spirit is always manifested by one gift—the gift of tongues. They have what to them is a meaningful experience, and then they make the grave mistake of universalizing it. Everybody, they say, must receive the same gift in order to be "spiritual." Their universalizing results in distorted interpretations of the Scriptures they use to prove their point. The problem of universalizing our experiences, however, is not limited to Pentecostals. Many of us, perhaps all of us, do it. We think that everybody else should believe and act the way we do. However, if our concept of the church came to pass, that is, if everybody were exactly like us, the body would not exist in its wholeness. The result would be similar to a body consisting of a monstrous eye or a monstrous ear (see 1 Cor 12:17). The wonderful variety essential for the functioning of the church as the body of Christ would be impossible.

A MEMBER: A FUNCTIONING PART OF THE BODY

Against this background, we turn to the main point. What does it mean to say you are a member of the church in terms of the Pauline image? Clearly it implies that you are a functioning part of the body of Christ. Each person has a gift or gifts to be used in cooperation with all the others. Just as an arm is meaningless and useless apart from the human body, who you are and what you do have significance only as they relate to the life and ministry of the church. It means that you are closely related to other members of the body—that you as a Christian are not a solo performer but part of a harmonious whole that depends for meaning on what everybody else is and what everybody else does. It means, as Paul pointed out in 1 Corinthians 12:14-26, that you need all the other members and that they all need you. It means that whatever your gift, however unspectacular and lowly, it is just as important, if not more important, than those gifts that attract the most attention. It means that if one member of the body hurts the whole body suffers.

One problem in American Christianity is that excessive individualism characterizes much of it. Many individuals proclaim, often with some arrogance, that they are not a part of the "institutional" church and that their relationship with God is private and personal, having nothing to do with other people. If there is anything to what we have been saying in the preceding pages, such a notion is patently erroneous and misses the whole point of the purpose of God in the world, which is to create a community of people who love one another. What does it mean to be a member of the church? It means you are a functioning part of a community.

OTHER IMAGES OF THE CHURCH

The image of the believer as a functioning member of the body is rich in implications. But other images also emphasize that an individual life has meaning in God's purpose only as it is related to other believers. In 1 Peter 2:5 we find the image of the believer as a building stone: "and like living stones, let yourselves be built into a spiritual house, to be a holy priesthood, to offer spiritual sacrifices acceptable to God through Jesus Christ." Here the totality of the Christian community is described in terms of the temple of Jewish worship. The temple is no longer a structure constructed by human hands. It is the people of God. Each member of the community is a stone in that holy building. Just as a literal building block has no meaning apart from its inclusion in a building and its contribution to the wholeness of that building, the meaning of the Christian's life comes only in relationship to other Christians. Together they constitute the holy place, the temple, in which the worship of God takes place.[2]

Another way of describing the church is by using the metaphor of a flock. In Acts 20:28 Paul is depicted as saying to the Ephesian elders, "Keep watch over yourselves and over all the flock, of which the Holy Spirit has made you overseers, to shepherd the church of God that he obtained with the blood of his own Son." This image of the church is found in other passages in the New Testament. It occurs at various points in the Old Testament as an image for Israel, the people of God.[3]

A related image is that of Jesus as the shepherd of the flock (John 10–11). In this connection we all remember the vivid illustration used by Jesus in Luke 15 of the shepherd who goes out to seek the sheep that has become separated from the flock. The image is not as powerful to us as it was to the people who first received the books of the Bible. They all knew about sheep and shepherds. They all knew how dangerous it was for a sheep to separate from the flock where it would be the helpless prey of its enemies. Furthermore, they were well acquainted with the responsibility of the shepherd to keep the flock together. They all interpreted the images when applied to the people of God in the light of their personal experience. The people of God are not individuals, separated and isolated from each other. Each person is part of a people who depend for their welfare on staying together under the guidance of their good Shepherd.

Family is also an image that gives insight into God's purpose for the church. All people who have placed their trust in God through Jesus are intimately related to each other as sisters and brothers (see, e.g., 1 John 2:9f.). God is the Parent, and Jesus is the Elder Brother. There are some families that, like some churches, are severely fragmented. However, the ideal of the church is to be like those closely knit families who love spending time together, who offer each other emotional support when needed, and who come to the aid of those who are suffering financially or in any other way.

DOES THE CHURCH SAVE?

Not only do our lives as believers have meaning only as they function in the context of the church, but our destiny also is wrapped up with that of all believers. The Roman Catholic Church teaches that there is no salvation outside the church. That is true, as will be pointed out below. The theology that stands behind the statement, however, is open to question. Along with most other Protestants, I do not believe that the church administers salvation through the sacraments, beginning with baptism. One basic problem with this idea is that it views the church as an entity over against the individual, rather than as a body formed by individuals.[4]

On the other hand, evangelical theology is distorted in the emphasis it puts on the individual. Individuals do make the decision for faith, but there is no salvation apart from the church. To be saved means that one is included in the church. The individual has no choice in this. It is God's doing.

Perhaps something else needs to be said by way of explication for those to whom this is a new idea. God's reality is not determined by the historical fragmentation of the church nor by our limited understanding of the extent of its boundaries. The redeemed community consists of everyone whom God includes and is not circumscribed by our prejudices. Arrogance is probably the most difficult sin for the Christian community. That arrogance is expressed in our assumptions about the boundaries of the redeemed community. We audaciously identify those who are in (which always includes us, of course) and those who are out. The only difference among us is that some of us make the boundaries a little more spacious than others. However, none of us can really understand the breathtaking sweep of God's ultimate purpose that we Christians come to know through Jesus of Nazareth.

The whole church will finally be redeemed. One of the eschatological images of the church is that of the bride of Christ being prepared for her marriage to the groom, that is, Christ (see Eph 5:25-27; Rev 19:7). Occasionally I see a church building with a sign that proclaims it as an "independent" church. I always hope that it is not too independent, for there is no special, segregated heaven for that church or for any group of churches. Our eternal destiny is tied to the destiny of the entire church. There is really no salvation outside the church, which I am using here as a term for the redeemed community. In the broad biblical sense, to be redeemed means not only that alienation between individuals and God is overcome, but also that people are no longer alienated from one another. To be redeemed in its fullest meaning is to be made a part of God's community. In this case, as in so many others, theology needs to walk the middle ground between two apparently opposing points of view.

GOD'S CHURCH AND THE HISTORICAL REALITY

As I wrote in an earlier chapter, God's purpose is to redeem a people who love God and in so doing create a community of people who love one another. That often seems to be a distant, unattainable, mocking goal in the light of the divisions that afflict humanity, including those who claim to be followers of Jesus. However, we can rejoice and take hope in the conviction that God's reality is not determined by the human inability to live out that reality.

Another important idea is that the community of people united in love for God and love for one another is to be a sign to the chaotic, divided world. The church is the evidence that points to the future toward which God is moving the whole universe. The Epistle to the Ephesians, the great book in the New Testament about the church, describes in cosmic terms God's purpose and the church's place in that purpose. God has not surrendered to the chaotic forces of evil with all their manifestations and consequences—hatred, prejudice, alienation, fear, and hopelessness. In Christ God is working to unite a shattered universe, to make the world whole (Eph 1:9-10). This is genuinely a dramatic concept.

As we survey what goes on about us—division, jealousy, ethnic hatred, war—how can we believe that God is working to overcome this alienation and unify the whole universe? Ephesians points to the church through which "the wisdom of God in its rich variety might now be made known to the rulers and authorities in the heavenly places" (Eph 3:10). In other words, the church is where the world will see the eternal purpose of God coming to reality in the world. God is bringing Jew (1:11-12) and Gentile (1:13) into one community and forming of them God's new people.[5] Jew and Gentile despised each other. Properly understood, Jesus' mission was to break down that "dividing wall of hostility" and "create in himself one new man in place of the two."[6]

Echoing that idea, Paul declared in Galatians 3:28, "There is no longer Jew or Greek, here is no longer slave or free, there is no longer male and female, for all of you are one in Christ Jesus." This is truly one of the peaks of the New Testament revelation. God created a new humanity for which the old divisions of race, status, and sex were irrelevant.

The petition in Jesus' great intercessory prayer recorded in John's Gospel underlines the importance of unity of the church in the world. There Jesus asks that subsequent believers "may all be one. As you, Father, are in me, and I am in you, may they also be in us, so that the world may believe that you have sent me" (17:21). Indeed, the unity of the church is a significant theme in John, no doubt due to the writer's concern about the increasing fragmentation of Christian communities with which he was acquainted.

It is also a major concern of the writer of 1 John, who sees the divisions being introduced into the churches by a gnostic-like variation of Christianity. Gnostics believed that they were redeemed by a special kind of religious knowledge. Because they associated evil with the material universe, they denied the reality of the Incarnation. They contended that the divine Christ never was human and, therefore, was not crucified. The author of the epistle saw correctly that a salvation by knowledge, any kind of knowledge, is extremely divisive. Furthermore, the denial of the crucifixion undercut the foundation of Christian community, which was God's love demonstrated in the death of Jesus for us. That love for us is expressed in our love for one another (1 John 4:7-12).

Already in "The Importance of the Church" we have called attention to the great importance of the unity of the church in Paul's thought. A case in point is the Epistle to the Philippians in which, early on in the letter, he exhorted the congregation to "be of the same mind, having the same love, being in full accord and of one mind" (2:2). What he meant by "mind" is clearly seen in his description of the mind of Christ (2:5ff.), that is, an attitude of humility, of self-giving. It did not mean that believers necessarily had to think in the same way about their theology or express it with the same terminology used by everybody else. Any two people who have thought through their own personal theology will differ with each other at various points. In order for it to be my theology I cannot blindly endorse what someone else says. No matter how much we may differ in our ideas, however, we can have the mind of Christ that enables us to live together in love.

THE SCANDAL OF DISUNITY

From this point of view, the great scandal of the gospel is the fragmentation of the church. It is no wonder that so many skeptics are repelled by the church. One of the recurring themes of the New Testament, heard from the pulpit over and over again, is that the Spirit of God changes lives. The most drastic change of all, according to what we preach, is that we become loving people. More often than not, however, the way we live our lives is a lie to what the New Testament teaches and what we preach. We reject people who do not say their theology the same way we say ours. Not only so, but we have been cruel and murderous toward them in the name of God. The temptation is to express our righteousness as religious zeal demonstrated especially in how militant we are against "heretics."[7]

Where there is unity, it is often not the unity given by the Spirit, but a harmony secured by suppressing our differences. This makes for a false, hollow, and sometimes even immoral unity. During the civil rights struggle in this country, one rationale for pastors not taking a stand for justice was the desire not to divide the church. As was true in Germany under Hitler, many people found sanctuary in a position of neutrality. As one prominent pastor in the South phrased it, "I am going down the middle of the road with Jesus." Needless to say, going down the middle of the road on controversial issues never caused anybody to be crucified. The suppression of our differences cannot express God-given unity.

What has been said about disunity in the church also applies to the chaos in Christianity today with competing churches of competing denominations claiming to represent the total truth about God. In my opinion, nothing more aptly describes the whole of Christianity represented by its various branches than the old fable of the blind men examining an elephant. Each one came up with a totally different description of the elephant, depending on which part he felt with his hands. As Paul wrote in 1 Corinthians 13:12, "For now we see in a mirror, dimly." That is true of all of us. Our knowledge is partial and imperfect, to say the least. I used to begin my classes by telling my students: "I believe in God. And I believe in the God who revealed himself in Jesus. Everything else is subject to modification, not because of my lack of faith in God, but because I am aware that my theology is very imperfect and always relatively immature."

I decided long ago that other Christians, i.e., people who have committed themselves to the God who came to us in Jesus, are not my enemies but my brothers and sisters. I also realize that the present fragmented historical situation does not represent God's reality. We live in a divided and often hostile, competing world of claims and counter claims made by various denominations and people. Although it was necessary to sever connections with my traditional roots, I am a Baptist and will remain a Baptist during this life. I am comfortable with many of the historic positions of Baptists—the priesthood of the believer, my freedom and that of others to practice religion according to the dictates of our hearts, the separation of church and state, and others. Nevertheless, Baptist churches are not the only ones that belong to the community of faith. Often God does not speak to me as clearly through Baptists in the South as he does through others of his children. I am thinking now of the Pope's recent emphasis on our responsibility to the poor in his visit to Mexico in contrast to the weak stance on some of the pressing social issues taken by many Baptist churches known to me.

We cannot escape from the historical situation in which we find ourselves, the result of 2000 years of controversies, divisions, and hostility. Even so, we can recognize that the present situation does not represent the vision of the church found in Paul, John, and others. We do not have to permit the contemporary situation to prevent us from being inclusive in our thinking and actions. We can continue to believe that God is moving us somehow toward the achievement of the divine purpose for his people. We can be inclusive rather than exclusive. To a great extent, we can transcend the divisions by reaching out to all brothers and sisters to the extent that this is possible. Also, we can exert our influence toward becoming what by God's grace we already are, that is, one people in Christ.

INACTIVE CHURCH MEMBERS

In conclusion, we will examine two practical applications of our discussion. Earlier we pointed out that the believer is first described as a member of the church (the body) in 1 Corinthians 12:12ff. As we have seen, this means that each believer is a functioning member of the body whose significance is found only in terms of its contribution, along with others, to the functioning of the whole body. The body is whole only as all constituent parts function properly.

This should cause us to raise questions about how we classify people as members of the church. Many who claim to be members of most churches are not functioning parts of the body as a whole. They fall into two categories. The first is what we term inactive church members. These are members of our churches today who have little or no relationship to the body or to the other members of the body. At best they show up for worship at Christmas or Easter and are not seen or heard from in the intervals. Some are never found in the assembly of their brothers and sisters at all. Granted, a person may attend church services regularly and still not be a good Christian when measured by the central criteria. Nevertheless, a minimal part of being a Christian, if what we have discussed is at all true, is the assembling of ourselves for worship and fellowship.

Apparently this was not a problem in New Testament times. The only adumbration of it is found in Hebrews, a writing probably addressed to Christians toward the end of the first century. They were a couple of generations removed from those heady, intense times of the beginning. The writer enjoins his readers not to be guilty of "neglecting to meet together, as is the habit of some" (10:25).

We can understand why it was not the problem in early Christian churches that it is in our churches today. Christianity was new. As is often the case with new movements, early believers were filled with excitement and enthusiasm. Acts tells of Christians who wanted to be together all the time, meeting daily (see 2:43-47). Also, joining the new movement was not something one did thoughtlessly. The price paid to be a follower of Christ in the world was often extreme. Christians constituted a tiny part of the vast Roman Empire and were commonly despised and under suspicion. Nobody had to explain to the earliest converts that becoming a believer was risky. Under such circumstances, people generally do not join a movement unless they are very committed to it. When they were baptized, new believers cut their ties to the pagan world and identified themselves with a struggling, misunderstood, often hated minority. This commitment was not undertaken lightly.

In our culture the opposite is true. It does not cost anything to become a member of the church in this country today. A person running for political office is helped by being identified with a Christian group. The fact that one is a member of a church is usually part of the campaign propaganda issued to influence the electorate to vote for an individual. I do not know much about other churches, but from personal experience I know that Baptist churches in general require less from a person claiming membership in them than does any civic organization in town. Many times the problem is exacerbated by our superficial evangelism. "All you have to do is believe. All that is required is that you step out for Jesus." These statements are typical of the appeals one hears in many congregations. It is true that trusting in Christ makes one a Christian, but that trust, properly understood from the perspective of the New Testament, involves a radical, fundamental change in life's values and loyalties.

Some churches today are never able to get even fifty percent of their members together to worship God on Sunday morning, much less involve them in living out their faith meaningfully in their home, work, and play. It seems logical to conclude that something should be done to confront people more sharply with their responsibility to Christ, the Lord of the church. People who display such an indifference to the welfare of the body of Christ should not be able to hide behind the fact that their names happen to appear on a church roll.

A RADICAL STEP

If I were in charge of a church, which I have never been as a Baptist minister and never want to be, I would plan to give members an opportunity periodically to examine what their initial decision meant. In Baptist circles, because of the emphasis on the "once saved, always saved" doctrine of our Calvinistic forebears, we place far too much weight on that initial decision. Whatever it means, it should be a "decision to decide" whose reality will be manifested in subsequent decisions that determine the authenticity of our commitment to Christ.

In order to emphasize this, I would like to see churches adopt a program that I heard another church had put in place. Every two or three years the churches could set aside a full month in which the question of each member's commitment to life in the fellowship of that church would be raised and reexamined. All the worship for that month would be shaped with that issue in mind. Also, I would put a blank book on the altar and request all those who desired to renew their commitment to be involved members of the congregation to write their names in an appropriate place.

Of course, as anyone can see, logistical problems would arise. Some people are physically unable to attend the services of the church. Others may be out of the community for the month. These matters, however, can be addressed so that all the people who make a renewed commitment to serve Christ in the fellowship of that body would constitute the functional roll of the church until the next month of renewed commitment. Perhaps this would get us closer to what Paul meant when he described believers as members of the body.

NONRESIDENT CHURCH MEMBERS

In the light of what the New Testament teaches about church membership, there is another anomaly that Baptist churches and other similar groups need to confront. I am talking about what we in our circles call nonresident church membership. The following is the kind of conversation that often takes place.

Church member to a new friend: "Are you a member of a church?"

Answer: "Yes, I am."

Church member: "Are you a member of a church here in Raleigh, North Carolina?"

Answer: "No, my church is in California."

Question: "How long have you lived in Raleigh?"

Answer: "About twelve years."

This illustrates the incongruity between the concept of church membership in the New Testament and the modern notion of what it means. The person from California is not and cannot be a member of the church in any New Testament sense. That person is not a functioning part of the body, a stone in the temple God erected as the dwelling place of the Spirit, a sheep in a flock, or a member of a family. The person's claim to be a church member is an absurdity. An individual with one arm can just as sensibly claim to have two arms, even though one of them is separated from the body.

A NON-NEW TESTAMENT PROBLEM

Once again, this is a non-New Testament situation. How were believers identified as members of a local congregation in the first century? This is another one of those questions for which the documents do not preserve an answer. We can be sure, however, that it was not because their names were on some church roll, a more modern development that in all likelihood did not exist at that time. The logical answer is that they became members of a congregation by being in the community. Christians baptized in Ephesus who moved to Corinth would become members of the Christian community in Corinth as soon as they arrived in the city. We can assume that Christians, upon moving to new places, would seek out and identify themselves with the local church immediately. When Paul addressed his letter to the church in Corinth, he was thinking of all Christians who lived in Corinth. The address of the letter is inclusive. The intended recipients are described as all people in Corinth who are saints (Christians) by virtue of their response to God's invitation (call) to become one of God's people (1 Cor 1:2). Paul addressed Romans "to God's beloved in Rome," further described as the people who were saints because of God's invitation (call), that is, to all believers in Rome (Rom 1:7). Remember also that individuals would only become privy to Romans by hearing it read in the congregation.

All the churches I am acquainted with make unrealistic membership claims. Their rolls are bloated not only by the names of totally inactive local residents but also by the names of people who have not lived in the community, sometimes for years. The churches thus contribute to the failure of those who are able to avoid their responsibilities as followers of Jesus Christ where they live. These people take shelter in their "membership" in their so-called home church. In my opinion, one of the policies of a church should be to give members who move to another community six months to identify with a congregation where they live. After that time they would know that they could no longer claim membership in the former church.

NOTES

[1] C. K. Barrett, *The First Epistle to the Corinthians*, Harper's New Testament Commentaries (New York: Harper & Row, 1993), 278.

[2] A more complete discussion of this idea takes place in another connection. I mention it here because it illustrates the point under discussion.

[3] See Isa 63:6; Jer 13:17; Zech 10:3, for example.

[4] This idea of the church as an institution over against the individual member is also common in non-Catholic churches, as we shall see. It is difficult for a group of people to grasp the basic fact that they are the church. The church is not a building or an organization. It is a community created by God.

[5] In this passage "we" refers to Jews, and "you" refers to Gentiles as is the case also in Eph 2:1-3.

[6] Ephesians 2:14-15. We have in this passage another powerful image. The church is God's new creation. The first creation has been splintered by evil, but the creative power of God is again at work bringing order out of chaos, as it was in the beginning.

[7] By definition, anybody who disagrees with us.

Women in the Church

The role of women in the church is a hotly debated issue in our time. Many churches take the position that women have no role in the official ministry of the church and should never be ordained. Some go to the extreme of not allowing women to teach groups that include men. On the other hand, an increasing number argue that women should be free to perform any of the functions traditionally limited to male members of the church. Due to the controversial nature of the issue, I give special consideration to the subject in this chapter.

THE INFLUENCE OF CULTURE

A prerequisite to good interpretation of Scripture is the recognition that the writers of Bible books were children of their times. What they knew of their universe and world was limited to the knowledge extant in their day. That has always been true. God gave neither those writers nor us the ability to transcend the culture and know what cannot be known in a particular time. The writers of the New Testament belonged scientifically and culturally to the first century and not to the twenty-first century. It is unfair to judge them by modern ideas and knowledge. People who have lived for more than seven decades, as I have, are aware that the notions we held in the 1940s and 1950s of the last century differ in many ways from those we hold today. For example, I am much more sensitive to discrimination based on race and sex than I was in my early years. Part of it has to do with the natural process of maturation, but much of it has to do with a change in my cultural context. I have been made more aware of the importance of certain issues than I used to be. You and I are children of our culture; so were the writers of both the Old and New Testaments.

An example of this is the cosmology of the Bible. The biblical writers lived prior to Copernicus and Galileo. They did not know that the earth was round or that it revolved around the sun. They held to the structure of a three-storied universe, with the heavens above and the netherworld beneath. For them the earth was the center of the universe. Later scientists like Galileo aroused intense hostility from religious authorities because what they discovered in their research differed from the "literal" meaning of Scripture. Religious leaders of Galileo's time held that the cosmology embraced by the writers of Scripture was true and that anything contrary to their views was wrong. Galileo is not the only scientist who has suffered because of differing with the assumptions of biblical writers. No matter how literally one interprets Scripture today, it would be difficult to find anyone who contends that the earth is flat or that it is the center of the universe, as people generally believed two thousand years ago.

THE BIBLE AND SLAVERY[1]

The institution of slavery was one aspect of the culture that conditioned the biblical writers. The practice of slavery was firmly rooted in Old Testament laws. Although strictly regulated, it was also accepted. However, it should be noted that the institution of slavery was ubiquitous, existing in all societies. Slavery was an extremely important part of the economic system of the world in which the earliest Christians lived, and it continued to be so until well into the nineteenth century. Thus, "Christian" slave owners in this country were able to find biblical texts to justify what we consider a barbaric practice. One of the most important texts used in the defense of slavery was Ephesians 6:5-9. It goes without saying that Paul, as a child of his generation, could not possibly conceive of a society without slavery, especially since that society was dominated by sin.[2]

Furthermore, he believed that the "parousia"[3] (the victorious return of the Lord) was about to take place. At that moment, the "kingdom of the world [would] become the kingdom of our Lord and of his Messiah" (Rev 11:15). This present, evil age was about to come to an end, supplanted by the reign of God who would correct all its evils. From Paul's perspective a Christian's socioeconomic circumstances in this life should not be of major concern since this life was temporary. God would soon intervene to bring about an eternal order of justice. Furthermore, in that new order where sin would be abolished, inequities in the status of its citizens would not exist. In the meantime, believers should remember that the God to whom they answered showed no partiality (Eph 6:9) and govern their conduct accordingly.[4] In other words, in God's coming kingdom Christian slaves would be on the same footing as their former masters.

A third factor helps explain early Christian views about the social order. Christians constituted a small minority of the population and were powerless to change the structures of society. It was impossible for that small, powerless group even to contemplate the possibility of changing the present social order, which they viewed as evil in any case. The toleration of the institution of slavery, therefore, was the result of cultural influences, eschatological theology, and possibilities of the times.

The moment arrived in human history, however, when those who called themselves Christian were no longer an insignificant minority in places like England and the United States. Then important ideas in the New Testament could have greater influence on the world. Paul did not advocate the abolition of slavery. Nevertheless, he expressed ideas that, carried to their logical conclusion, would destroy the institution of slavery. He affirmed that master and slave were one in the church and that God was no respecter of people (Gal 3:28; Eph 6:9; Phlm 15-16). In Christ there was neither slave nor free. Slaves were just as important to God as masters.

These Christian ideas, challenging the basic presuppositions and attitudes of society and transforming human relationships, were understood in later times to constitute the genuine word of God to the people. At that time, the biblical justification used by slave owners was considered contrary to the will of God. The revolutionary concepts in Ephesians 6:9, Galatians 3:28, and Philemon 15-17, along with many others found in the teachings of Jesus and elsewhere, became an important biblical basis for the rejection of slavery by Christians like William Wilberforce, an important leader in the movement to do away with the slave trade and abolish slavery in the British possessions, and David Livingstone, the great Scottish missionary to Africa. Biblical texts used by slave owners to justify their barbaric practice were not believed valid by the people committed to abolishing the business of buying and selling other humans.

WOMEN IN NEW TESTAMENT TIMES

In order to interpret New Testament passages about women, we need an understanding of the social context in which early Christians lived. As was true of the institution of slavery, the patriarchal structure of Jewish society was not unique. Males dominated the social order in every culture, whether Roman or Greek, Jewish or pagan. Thus, the structure of family and society that gave dominance to the male was neither uniquely Jewish nor Christian. In other words, it was not inspired of God. All the writers of the Bible along with the other peoples of their time lived in a society in which women were subservient to men.

The standing of women differed, of course, from society to society. Nevertheless, women were uniformly of secondary importance in the power structures and with rare exceptions were totally dependent on men. In Judaism women had no standing before the law. Their testimony was not valid in court. If they did not have a man to act and speak for them, they were helpless, having no recourse to the legal system. One of the limiting factors of the world of the first century was the complete economic dependence of women on men. There are a few biblical references to women who were engaged in business activities.[5] Generally speaking, however, the only socially approved vocation open to most women was that of wife and mother. The situation of women whose husbands died and who had no son or other male relative on whom to depend could be tragic indeed.

Things are vastly different in our generation. In our society, all vocations open to men are also theoretically open to women. Women can provide financially for themselves, and many of them do. They are not as dependent on men as they once were. In the last century, laws, including the constitution itself, were changed to guarantee women equal status before the law. This development has given women the opportunity to claim more roles in society. The changes, legal and otherwise, of the twentieth century afforded the essential context for us to be able to progress more rapidly in our ideas about the status of women.

The improvement in the status of women has also made it imperative for us to interpret differently what the New Testament says about them. During earlier days when the status of women was severely less than it is today, it was much easier for people to feel comfortable with the patriarchal system that permeates the Bible. Where the Bible reflects the patriarchal system of the culture, it is not Christian, neither is it revelation. It simply expresses the commonly held ideas of all societies—pagan, Jewish, or Christian—that kept women subservient to men. Such passages affirm rather than challenge the dominant culture of the first century. There are, however, biblical insights that do challenge the dominant and sinful culture. In my opinion, they are the ones that should govern our thinking about the role of women in the church, as well as other matters.

EPHESIANS 5:21-33

Ephesians 5:21-33 is a good example. In it Paul deals with the concepts of submission and authority. He talks about women being "subject" to their husbands and husbands being the "head" of the wife. Most of us who are conscious of the history of discrimination against women feel uncomfortable with the use of these terms. Even in my most insensitive days I do not believe I ever stated that the husband was the head of the wife. Although the writer uses traditional terms, notice, however, that he redefines those concepts in Christian terms and gives new meaning to them. A woman is to be submissive to her husband, but that injunction is set in the context of a general exhortation (5:21). *All the members, male and female, are to be submissive to one another!* In other words, it is a rephrasing of the demand of Jesus that his followers be servants of all. Submission in the Christian vocabulary does not mean subservience, as it is often understood. In any relationship, the Christian approach demands that we put the welfare of others ahead of our own. That is what Christian submission involves.

The way some people interpret this and other passages, however, excludes any man from the possibility of being a great Christian by Jesus' own definition. If the greatest of his followers is the one who is servant of all (Mark 10:43, 44), only a woman can qualify, since men cannot be submissive to women.

In the same way the concept of authority is reinterpreted. The passage reads: "For the husband is the head of the wife *just as* Christ is the head of the church" (5:23, my italics). Christ is the pattern of authority. His is not the authority that demands. It is that of the lover who gives. It is that of the Suffering Servant who died for his church. That kind of authority is the most powerful of all because it claims the heart. In essence, the injunctions both to husband and wife can be interpreted to mean essentially the same thing. Thus, submission and authority both produce the same results and issue in the same actions.

In the ideal marriage husband and wife will have the same attitude because both will put the welfare of the other ahead of their own.

WOMEN MINISTERS IN THE OLD TESTAMENT

Most ministerial vocations were closed to women in Israel and Judaism. By definition priests were male descendants of Aaron, and Levites were the male descendants of Levi. In neither case did any criteria necessarily come into play except that of genealogy and gender. Priests did not have to be moral in order to exercise their vocation. Neither was the morality of the high priest necessarily a factor, although he presided over the highest and holiest ritual of Judaism. According to Jewish belief, he was the one who came closest to God when he entered the holiest place on the Day of Atonement.

Under the Syrians and Romans, the high priests owed their position to the power of the conquerors. They were chosen because of their desire to cooperate and compromise and their willingness to outbid rivals for the position. In the history of Judaism the high priest at times was more pagan in beliefs and practices that he was Jewish. He could even be the leader of the opposition party that wanted to adopt the practices of the larger pagan society. If successful, that would have brought about the demise of the Jewish religion, at least in the form that we know it.

There was one ministry, however, that was open to women. *Women could be prophets!* Prophets were unique in that they were chosen and called specifically by God. Questions of sex, age, status in society, or occupation were irrelevant. God through the Spirit exercised total freedom from rules and restrictions in the choice of prophets, calling all kinds of people to exercise the prophetic gift. These people, especially endowed by God's Spirit, received the contemporary word of God and were responsible for delivering it to the people. It was God's message to them for that hour and that situation. As we shall see in our discussion of ministry in the New Testament, the prophetic ministry may have been the most important of all. Unlike the case of the priest and the Levite, the prophet's relationship to God, commitment to God, and willingness to make great sacrifices for God were the qualifications of the office.

True, male prophets greatly outnumber females in the Old Testament; nevertheless, a few prophetesses are mentioned. Miriam, the sister of Moses, is called a prophetess (Exod 15:20), and Micah names her along with Aaron and Moses as a leader of the children of Israel (6:4). Deborah, a prophetess (Judg 4:4), was for a time the leader of the Israelites in their struggle against the Canaanites. When the book of the Law, perhaps Deuteronomy, was discovered in the temple, King Josiah sent emissaries to find out what God had to say about it. They went to Huldah, the prophetess (2 Kgs 22:14), who evidently was regarded as the person through whom God was speaking during that time. In the New Testament Anna is called a prophetess (Luke 2:36). Obviously Luke thought of her as belonging in that line of Spirit-inspired men and women through whom God had periodically addressed the people. As we have seen, female prophets in the Old Testament are few in number, but the examples suffice to demonstrate that the gift of the Spirit was not limited by gender. The Spirit of God could endow women or men with the capacity to receive and proclaim the word of God to the people. Unlike so many priests and high priests, the prophets were close to God and were totally committed to the ministry to which they were called.

WOMEN IN THE GOSPELS

To begin with, we should note that women, named and nameless, are prominent in the gospel story. Sisters Mary and Martha, Mary the mother of Jesus, Mary Magdalene, the woman at the well, and the woman who anointed the feet of Jesus were among those who followed and supported Jesus in his ministry. Even among the Gospel writers, there is a difference in the emphasis placed on women. Joseph is the main player in Matthew's account of the birth of Jesus, whereas Luke makes Mary the central figure. Indeed, Luke gives special attention to women in his account of the ministry of Jesus and in the life of the church depicted in Acts. This is expressed in the stories about Elizabeth, Anna, the widow at Nain, the penitent harlot, the ministering women from Galilee, Martha and Mary, the bent woman, and the women in the parables about the lost coin and unjust judge. In Acts the same emphasis is illustrated in the references to Tabitha, Lydia, Priscilla, and the four daughters of Philip.

According to John 4, Jesus disregarded all the barriers and conventions designed to "keep women in their place" to minister to the Samaritan woman. In the story of the woman taken in adultery, Jesus defended her against her self-righteous male accusers (John 8:1ff.). It is noteworthy that in a number of places Jesus takes the side of women. All the texts used by those who argue for the subservience of women to men come from books outside the Gospels. True, the Twelve were all male, but we need to understand some of the factors involved. It is commonly believed that the Twelve represented the original patriarchs (all men) and, thus, the whole of Israel. Jesus was bringing into being the new Israel. Thus, they would have to be men as a parallel to the patriarchs. Furthermore, the kind of life to which the people traveling with Jesus were subjected was hardly what women were expected to accommodate.

It is important to notice that the Twelve, without exception, acted as cowards when the crisis came in Jesus' life. The only friends at the crucifixion of Jesus, according to the witness of the New Testament, were women who had followed him during his ministry (Matt 27:55 and parallels). The women were also there when he was buried (Matt 27:61; Luke 23:55f.). Furthermore, the New Testament account says that women were the first to go to the tomb and the first to receive an appearance from the Risen Lord. They were ones chosen to tell the good news to the disciples. Therefore, women had the honor of being the first preachers (Mark 16:7). According to Luke, the male disciples reacted to their story with the kind of disrespect to which women have become accustomed (Luke 24:11).

WOMEN MINISTERS IN ACTS

Now, what about the subject of women's participation in the various official ministries of churches? We have already noted that Anna is called a prophetess, and, as the text says, she spoke of Jesus "to all who were looking for the redemption of Jerusalem" (Luke 2:38). She proclaimed God's message to men and women. Likewise, we read in Acts 21:9 that Philip "had four unmarried daughters who had the gift of prophecy."

Although her role is not given a specific title, it is clear that Prisca (Priscilla) played an important part in Paul's ministry. In Acts 18:2 we are told how Paul met Aquila and Prisca after they had arrived in Corinth. In this, the first mention of the couple, the husband's name is placed first. In subsequent references, however, Prisca's name is always placed ahead of her husband's, indicating that her role in their ministry was of greater importance. An interesting reference is found in Acts 18:26 where we are told that Prisca and Aquila invited Apollos to their home to explain the gospel to him. Prisca taught Apollos! In Romans 16:3 Paul calls Prisca and Aquila those "who work with me in Christ."

That is about as specific as Paul ever was in identifying the role of any of his companions in ministry, male or female.

A DECISIVE INSIGHT

In my opinion the two most important texts found outside the Gospels to support the emancipation of women are Galatians 3:28 and Acts 2:17. In the Galatians passage, Paul soared above the common thinking of the cultures of his day when he made a statement that must have startled his contemporaries: "There is no longer Jew or Greek, there is no longer slave or free, there is no longer male or female; for all of you are one in Christ Jesus" (Gal 3:28). This means that in Jesus Christ the structures of human society became totally meaningless. Society's divisions are always an expression of its prejudices and power structure. Its divisions depend solely on who is in control and who dictates public opinion. Of course, the group determining the structures always puts itself in the most favored and elevated spot.

Such divisions are determined by the color of the skin, by the size of the purse, by the achievements of the intellect, and by the gender of the power group. Paul mentioned three that were important in his day: ethnic background (Jews, Greeks), economic situation (slave, free), and gender (male, female). If Jews were doing the dividing, they were the superior group. In any case, slaves were considered the lowest group, and women were invariably the lesser gender. Paul declared that the radical transformation experienced by the Christian community abolished those distinctions. All that mattered was that the individual have a relationship to God through Jesus Christ. In the Christian community, all people were on the same footing. All were servants of each other; power was no longer an issue. Men were no longer superior to women. All believers, male and female, were members of the family and, therefore, brothers and sisters in Christ. Gender was erased as an issue in the Christian community. Men and women had the same responsibility for each other and for the community.

The tragedy is that the average Christian community comes far short of attaining the ideal of a classless society. Too often the structures of culture determine those of the Christian community. As we know too well, in the interest of protecting those cultural structures, some Christians can always find biblical texts that they interpret to support their arguments. The call of the church has always been to be "in the world but not of the world." However, it is often difficult to see much difference between the values of the contemporary Christian congregation and that of the society in which it is found. The church too often reflects the prejudices of the culture in which it is embedded. Paul perceived that the earthly Christian community, the community of the last days, was called on to be a model of the eternal reality that lay in its future.

THE IMPACT OF PENTECOST

The second important text, in my opinion, is Acts 2:17, a quotation from Joel 2:28. We discussed Pentecost in a previous chapter when we noted that the pouring out of the Spirit on the nascent church signified a beginning of the last days. The manifestation of that reality lay in the fact that all God's people were recipients of the Spirit. The fact that all of them were able to receive and transmit the message of God, to prophesy, indicated that they all received the Spirit.

Prior to this dawning of the last days, the prophets had been few. The gift of prophecy was bestowed on a select group of people before that time. On the other hand, in the eschatological community, the community of the last days, every believer would have the gift of the Spirit according to Joel 2:28, the text cited by Peter. [6] This meant that any of them could be endowed with the gift of prophecy. There was to be no distinction with regard to gender; the sons and daughters would prophesy. Any of them could be a preacher. Let it be noted again that the highest expression of the Spirit's presence in pharisaic Jewish theology was the gift of prophecy.[7] If prophecy, the supreme gift of the Spirit, was available to all, no other gift was to be denied any of God's children. There was to be no distinction between male and female as far as the capacity to serve God was concerned.

SHOULD CHRISTIAN WOMEN WEAR VEILS?

If one believes as Paul did that all believers received the Spirit when they first confessed faith in Jesus, then one must believe, provided one's theology is coherent, that any Christian may receive any of the gifts of the Spirit, including the gift of prophecy. This theological principle lies behind what Paul wrote in 1 Corinthians 11:1-16.

Another underlying assumption of the passage is that believers would participate in the public worship of the church when inspired to do so by the Spirit. That is, prior to assembling for worship the members of the Corinthian church did not know who would lead in prayers or proclaim God's contemporary word to the church. Similarly, in the liturgy of the Jewish synagogue the choice of individuals to do certain things, such as read Scripture or deliver the sermon or homily, apparently was made during the assembly itself. However, from what we can gather the worship of the Corinthian congregation was more unrehearsed that that of the synagogue. The leader of worship did not select the person who would pray or proclaim God's word as was done in the synagogue; the Spirit did. All members were free to participate if they felt inspired to do so by the Spirit.

In 1 Corinthians 11:5 Paul went to the heart of his concern in this passage when he stated that "any woman who prays or prophesies with her head unveiled disgraces her head." Two important points are clear in this statement: (1) Paul assumed that women would play a role in the congregational worship of the church by leading in prayer or preaching; and (2) he thought that it was shameful for a woman to pray or prophesy unveiled. In other words, he was concerned about what he considered appropriate attire for women.[8]

All kinds of questions arise in this connection. Why did Paul make so much of this in the letter to the Corinthians and nowhere else in his writing? What tradition of female dress determined his concept of a properly clad woman? Did the customs in Corinth demand that respectable women wear a veil in public? Or, much more likely, was he seeking to impose a Jewish custom prevalent among Semitic people, as it continues to be to this day?

Our primary reason for calling attention to this passage is to show that women did play a part in public worship in Corinth and that Paul assumed their participation. However, some aspects of the case Paul made for wearing a veil in worship call for a brief comment. He used three arguments to make his point. First, he argued from creation. The husband, he declared, is the head of his wife (11:3). In this case head means origin and the statement is based on the second creation story found in Genesis 2, which states the woman was created from man. However, in the first creation story (Gen 1:26), we read that God created both male and female and that both were created in the image of God. This weakens Paul's argument that the male is created in God's image and the woman is a reflection of the man (1 Cor 11:7). According to the first Genesis passage, the woman is not assigned a derivative or secondary status in creation. Even if one uses the second story, as Paul did, it is difficult to see the logic in the argument that a woman should be veiled because she was created from man.

Paul did make an important observation when he affirmed that redemption played a significant role in the relationship of men and women. In 1 Corinthians 11:11 he wrote, "Nevertheless, in the Lord [that is, in the Christian community] woman is not independent of man or man independent of woman." This is in accord with Paul's statement in Galatians 3:28: "There is no longer Jew or Greek, there is no longer slave or free, there is no longer male and female; for all of you are one in Christ Jesus."

Paul used two other arguments in his attempt to convince the Corinthian women that they ought not to cut their hair and should wear veils. The first is that nature teaches us that women should not cut their hair (1 Cor 11:14). Obviously this argument is not convincing. Although more men are bald than women, baldness is not an exclusive male phenomenon. Furthermore, a large percentage of men are endowed by nature with as much hair as women have. The last argument is based on custom (1 Cor 11:16). For women to wear veils is the customary practice.

Many biblical literalists argue against women participating in public worship. However, the great majority of them do not believe that modern women should wear veils. It is difficult to understand how people who claim to be literalists can deny that Paul allowed women to speak in the assembled congregation, which is very clear in the text, or fail to believe that what Paul wrote about veils is not binding.

DID PAUL CONTRADICT HIMSELF?

This leads us to a consideration of 1 Corinthians 14:33b-35, one of the proof texts often cited by those who would limit women's activities in the church. In this text women are commanded to keep silent in the church. The problem presented by this text jumps out, however, even to the casual reader of 1 Corinthians. According to the general interpretation of this passage, what Paul said is apparently a violent contradiction of the assumption underlying 1 Corinthians 11:1-16 and cries out for an explanation. Having allowed for the contribution of women to the worship of the church if they were properly clothed, did Paul blatantly contradict himself in the same letter by taking the position that women were not to speak in the church at all? Scholars have suggested several solutions to the problem. The one outlined by Charles Talbert is the most convincing to me.[9] He concludes that verses 34-35 may have been a quotation by Paul of a position taken by some Corinthian men.[10]

Biblical writers did not use punctuation marks in their writing as we do today. Modern editors of the text added the periods, commas, quotation marks, and other marks of punctuation in the translations. On occasion, we have no doubt that we are dealing with a quotation. Nevertheless, often the decision that a passage is a quotation is more difficult to make.[11] Paul's exclamation (14:36), which follows the passage in question, may indicate that the preceding is a quotation: "What! Did the word of God originate with you, or are you the only ones it has reached?" Two aspects of this statement are important. "What!" indicates Paul's negative reaction to the preceding verses. We often use the interjection in the same sense. Furthermore, "only ones" is the translation of a word in the masculine gender. It could refer to men, or a group of men and women, but never to women alone. So, it cannot be Paul's response to the claims of the women. It refers to those who opposed the freedom of women to speak in the church. Those who use 1 Corinthians 14:34-35 to argue against women preaching make the mistake that Paul was attempting to correct in the church of Corinth.

PHOEBE, THE DEACON

Diakonos is a Greek word meaning "servant." We often translate the noun as "minister" and the verb as "to minister." It is a term Jesus used to describe himself. Of course, all Christians are servants or ministers. But the term can also be used specifically to refer to helping ministries in the Christian community. As the years passed, evidently the word became institutionalized more and more and was applied to a specific office in the church that we call "deacon" (Phil 1:1). The idea in the New Testament is always that of a helping ministry. One interesting and important note is that the only "deacon" specifically named in the letters of Paul is a woman called Phoebe. Paul wrote Romans 16:1-2 to commend Phoebe, a "deacon of the church at Cenchreae" (v. 1), to his readers.

People opposed to women serving as deacons in the church contend that the word describing Phoebe should be translated "servant." That translation, however, is arbitrary. There is no reason other than prejudice for understanding the word as "servant" in this context. The fact that Paul took special pains to recommend Phoebe to the church indicates that she had a special and important leadership role in the church she had served. He used the term to describe that relationship. This leaves us in the dark about Phoebe's specific duties, but that is true of every use of *deacon* in a more institutionalized sense in the New Testament.

WOMEN IN THE PASTORALS

The most explicit teachings for the subordination of women to men in the Christian community are found in 1 and 2 Timothy, two of the Pastoral Epistles, and outside the Pastorals in 1 Peter. The interpreter needs to keep two major facts in mind in the attempt to understand these letters. First, the overwhelming number of New Testament scholars believes that an admirer of Paul rather than Paul himself wrote the Pastorals. There are several reasons for this. The oldest manuscript of Paul's epistles does not contain the Pastorals.[12] Moreover, Marcion, a lover of Paul, did not include them in his canon (c. AD 140).[13] They are not quoted explicitly in the extant literature until AD 180. However, the most telling arguments relate to the fact that the theology and language of the Pastorals is unlike that of other Pauline epistles. Furthermore, the problems confronted in the Pastorals indicate a date for them later than Paul.[14]

Whatever we conclude about the question of authorship, we need to recognize several important issues in order to understand and interpret the Pastorals. One is that we confront in them a situation different from almost anything we meet in most other New Testament books. The problems confronted in the letters are similar to those later posed by Gnosticism, a movement that presented a grave threat to orthodox Christianity in the second century.

Two aspects of the heresy are relevant to understanding what the Pastorals say about women. First, some gnostic groups adopted asceticism, which expressed itself in a rejection of sex and marriage (see 1 Tim 4:1-5). In 1 Timothy the argument is that, rather than it being an evil institution, through marriage and having children the woman finds the place God has for her in the human family (1 Tim 2:15; 4:3; 5:14; Titus 2:3ff.). In the second place, the heresy apparently had a great appeal to women. Evidently the writer concluded that women were especially susceptible to the heretical doctrines and that their role in the Christian community needed to be strictly defined to keep them and the churches out of trouble (1 Tim 2:9ff; 2 Tim 3:6-7).

Similar teachings are found in 1 Peter 3:1-7, where women are urged to be submissive to their husbands. Here the context is evangelistic. The writer believed that women who had a right relation with their pagan husbands could win them to faith in Christ if they conducted themselves in accord with the contemporary social mores (v. 1). Following this and in the same passage, the writer also says, "Do not adorn yourselves outwardly by braiding your hair, and by wearing gold ornaments or fine clothing" (v. 3). In the instructions to women in 1 Timothy 2:9 we find the same emphasis. People who interpret verses instructing women to submit to their husbands as the literal word of God for every period and every culture generally have no trouble ignoring the advice against wearing cosmetics and jewelry found in the same passages. Apparently they regard adornment as a culturally conditioned prohibition. If part of the passage is the word of God *for all times*, how can one say that the rest of the same passage is a cultural matter and no longer valid?

Women are commanded to keep silent in the church (1 Tim 2:9ff.). This is contrary to the belief that in the new age of the Spirit anyone is capable of receiving the gift of prophecy. It creates classes in the church based on sex that are no different from the gender-oriented divisions of pagan society rejected by Paul in Galatians 3:28.

THE PASTORALS: DEACONS AND BISHOPS

The partial emancipation of women in a modern society such as ours has caused alarm in many Christian circles. Insecure because of so much uncertainty in a time when rapid change is the norm and in a culture in which people often abuse their freedom, many people have advocated turning back the clock to an idealized age in the past. Nothing seems to be nailed down. So much seems out of hand. Some people think that the emancipation of women has been a large contributor to the evils of our society. "If we could just put women back in their rightful place," they say, " their God-ordained place, fulfilling the role they have fulfilled in most of human history, then much of what is wrong with our world would be corrected."

The interesting aspect of it all is that the situation seems similar to the one the Pastorals confronted many years ago. At that time, the world seemed out of control. Dangerous doctrine and practices were proliferating, posing a genuine threat to the purity of the gospel. The response to this in the "orthodox" Christian churches was the increase in the power of the clergy, the development of creeds, and the formation of the canon of the New Testament, a process that continued for a lengthy period of time. That is, in a time of confusion and unrest, the response was an assertion of authority, including the authority of men over women and clergy over laity.

In the Pastorals we can see the beginning of the change to a hierarchically constructed church. The elders or bishops had the responsibility for being the centers of authority in the churches (cf. 1 Tim 5:17). Titus was given the responsibility of "appointing" elders in the churches of Crete (Titus 1:5). This is certainly not democratic church government advocated by many free churches. Titus was to be the authoritative voice in the region (Titus 2:1-10). Timothy was to exercise his oversight of the choice of bishops and deacons, guided by the instructions laid down by the apostle (1 Tim 3:1 f.). Thus, we see a hierarchy beginning to take shape, with several layers of authority. The intention was to preserve the gospel from the distortions of gnostic-like teachings. Some believed there had to be an authoritative center of control and a source of authoritative teachings for the church. Thus, we see the foundations laid for the Roman Catholic view of the church's role in Scripture interpretation.

The clear implication of 1 Timothy 3:2 is that the choice of bishops is limited to males. With regard to the function of deacon, however, the situation was different. In 1 Timothy the characteristics sought in deacons are set forth in some detail (3:8-13). We cannot be sure how the office began, nor can we trace the stages of its development. What is clear is that when 1 Timothy was written, the office of deacon had developed as a defined and official ministry of the church. Most of the passage is a discussion of the character and life of men chosen to be deacons. First Timothy 3:11, however, contains characteristics desired in "the women." The AV (King James Version) translates *gunaikas*, the generic word for "women," as "wives." This is a permissible but arbitrary rendition of the word. It is more likely that the translation is "women" and that the remarks are addressed to female deacons in the church.

There are two reasons for this. First, the characteristics enumerated are not those one would expect to find in a list of virtues related specifically to the role of wife. Rather the virtues are parallel to those in the list for male deacons found immediately above. In other words, they seem to be more appropriate in describing the attributes of women selected to serve in the same role. The second reason is that women deacons apparently were essential to the ministry of the church in early times. As early as AD 112 in the letter of Pliny, governor of Bithynia, to the emperor Trajan there is evidence of the existence of women deacons. In the third century a document describes the role of women deacons in baptisms of women, visitation of the sick, and visits to pagan homes where the woman was a believer. There were some ministries that men simply could not have performed in those areas. Let it be noted that the role of deacon in the early churches had nothing of the character that it has assumed in some contemporary churches. It was not an authoritative, decision-making office, but a helping ministry.

CONCLUSION

My argument here has been that we must interpret the early writings of the Christian church in the context of the times in which they were written. Everybody agrees that women and men are different. Disagreement among us is caused by the ways various individuals understand the nature of how men and women are different. In my early years of ministry, my wife would not have dreamed of wearing long pants to attend a church service. In American society in those days, wearing trousers was restricted to men, at least in our southern culture. At the same time in Chinese culture the opposite was true. So much of what we believe distinguishes females from males relates to the existing and changing social code. In my judgment, the important texts are not the ones that conform to a first-century social code. Rather, they are the ones that reinterpret or criticize the existing code in the light of Christian values. A hundred years from now historians will put the present generation's disagreements about the role of women in the context of the fears, ideals, problems, and struggles of this generation. They will treat the efforts to suppress women as we treat the slavery issue—wrong although the Bible offers texts that can be used to justify the practice.

However, as we read the New Testament, occasionally one insight grips us and causes us to see it as central to our understanding of what it means to be a Christian. I am convinced that the pivotal text comes from the Lord of the church himself: "Whoever wants to be first must be last of all and servant of all" (Mark 9:35). With regard to the role of women in the church and its ministry, in my opinion two texts are central, i.e., Galatians 3:28 and Acts 2:17. In the books of the New Testament, such as the Pastorals and 1 Peter, I see writers struggling with the grave issues of their times and giving what they believed to be the best counsel to the churches in their environment as they confronted these problems. However, I do not understand that all their ideas are pertinent to the churches in every age.

From my point of view the ideal Christian church is one where all are bound together in love, where everybody's efforts are exerted for the welfare of everybody else, and where the distinctions of race, class, or gender are irrelevant to relationships or gifts for ministry.

NOTES

[1] Some of the biblical texts used by supporters of slavery to justify the practice are found in the same passages as texts used by people today to justify their views about women. However, it would be difficult to find even a biblical literalist who would justify the barbaric practice of slavery.

[2] This assumes that Paul wrote Ephesians, an assumption disputed by many New Testament scholars.

[3] Parousia is the Greek term used in the New Testament to designate the event we usually refer to as the second coming.

[4] The small book of Philemon gives Paul's view about the proper relationship between a Christian slave owner and his slave. They were brothers.

[5] See Prov 31:16, 24; Acts 5:1; 16:14; 18:2-3.

[6] From the point of view of New Testament writers, the last days began with the coming of the Spirit after the ministry of Jesus.

[7] The Sadducees did not accept the prophetic books as authoritative Scripture.

[8] We all agree that one's sex is an important aspect of who one is. Being a woman is different from being a man. The question about which people often disagree has to do with how that difference is expressed. Even in our society, until recently, women were expected to dress in a way that distinguished them from men. Only in recent years have women felt that they could wear the kinds of clothes men wear. As a child of his times, Paul felt that women should clothe themselves differently from men. Women should cover their heads with veils, while men should not. The majority of Americans do not agree with this mandate no matter where they find themselves on the theological scale.

[9] Charles H. Talbert, *Reading Corinthians: A Literary and Theological Commentary on 1 and 2 Corinthians* (New York: Crossroad, 1987), 91ff.

[10] Other passages where Paul evidently quoted from the letter the Corinthians wrote to him are 1 Cor 6:12, 13; 7:1; 8:1; 10:23.

[11] The same would be true about periods, question marks, commas, etc.

[12] The manuscript is P46, produced around AD 200. One cannot be dogmatic about this conclusion because manuscripts were often damaged during handling.

[13] Marcion's canon is the known earliest attempt to define the body of authoritative New Testament writings. From his point of view, of the early writers, only Paul had the right understanding of the incarnation. Marcion had gnostic-like beliefs and was condemned as a heretic.

[14] Those who wish to read about this issue in detail should consult a good scholarly commentary or Bible dictionary.

Ministry in the New Testament

It should be clear from the first chapter of this book that my intention is not to treat any one subject exhaustively. This is certainly true about the following discussion of the ministry. There are good books that deal with the subject at length. I plan to use what is common knowledge as the context in which to present my own conclusions about New Testament teachings of ministry as understood in some first-century churches. Also, as is true with my previous discussions, I am most concerned about the relevance of the New Testament understanding of ministry to our practice of ministry today.

JESUS AS MINISTER

The proper starting place for achieving an understanding of our own ministry in the world today is the ministry of Jesus. He must always be the model for the ministers who seek to follow him. Minister (*diakonos*) is an important word in the life and teachings of Jesus. To us the term is rather high-sounding. For example, we use it to refer to important people in government. It is also considered one of the more respectable terms to apply to a pastor.

In the Greco-Roman world of the early church, however, *diakonos* was far from a respectable word. It literally meant "servant" and described individuals doing menial tasks. People in Hellenistic society did not aspire to be considered in the same class as the people who waited on tables. They wanted to be the ones who were waited on. Since *diaconos* described an individual in the servant class, therefore, individuals who belonged to the higher levels of Hellenistic society would not want that word used to describe them.

Jesus' use of this term to describe himself and those who would follow him is another indication that in his community the world's categories are turned upside down. Those considered to be in one of the lowest classes of human society according to the world's standards are the most important members of his group. A disciple strives for a life of serving. Jesus did not merely call on others to be servants; he led the way and established the model of servanthood for us to emulate. "I am among you as one who serves," he said (Luke 22:27). Throughout his life he exemplified the characteristics of a true servant.

According to this model, the welfare of others must take precedence over our own welfare. Our ambitions, needs, and desires take second place to our desire for the good of other people. Indeed, the ambition of the true servant is the exact opposite of the ambitions of most people. Self-promotion, self-aggrandizement, and the satisfaction of one's personal desires are incongruous with the attitude of the genuine servant. Jesus' example of service shows the failure of so many of us who claim to be his servants—as preachers, as missionaries, as denominational leaders. Far too often in the history of Christianity, leaders have exploited followers for their own welfare. We ignore the dictum set forth by the Lord of the church: "whoever wishes to become great among you must be your servant, and whoever wishes to be first among you must be slave [the lowest social class] of all" (Mark 10:43b-44).

The concept of authority, thus, is radically changed for the church. It is not the authority that demands, that insists on obedience to one's superior. Rather, it is the authority that claims the heart—the authority of love. It is uncalculating love—totally self-giving, unceasingly concerned for the welfare of others, and joyful in helping others in need. Wherever authority is rightly understood in the Christian community, whether that of bishop, pastor, or husband, it must be understood in this fashion. What is important is not how high our position is.[1] It is how effectively we use the opportunities we have for the good of others.

AN UNCLEAR PORTRAIT

As with much of early church life, the picture of ministry in those churches is far from clear. We know most about the church in Jerusalem as depicted in the book of Acts, the churches addressed by the Pastoral Epistles, and the church in Corinth. There are hints in other places. Nevertheless, the exact shape of the ministry, even in the churches we know most about, is once again far from clear. What ministers were called in a given church, the number of them deemed necessary, the determination of the tenure of their service, the criteria churches used in their selection, and how churches chose ministers are largely unknown. Furthermore, we know nothing at all about the majority of the churches that must have existed at that time. We do know, however, about the kinds of ministries that were deemed essential.

Whatever we conclude about the individual types of ministries in the New Testament, we note that there are some categories of ministries that the churches have always found essential. The first is the ministry of the word. Paul's lists of ministers include the apostles, prophets, evangelists, pastors, and teachers (Rom 12:6-8; 1 Cor 12:28-30). Then there is the ministry of helping or service mentioned by Paul in Romans 12:7. He also refers to the charismatic gifts of contributing, giving aid, and doing acts of mercy (Rom 12:8), which could be understood as specialized categories of the helping ministry. Another category of ministry is found in 1 Corinthians 12:28 where the apostle mentions the gift of administration.

In 1 Peter the author divides gifts into two categories with no mention of specific ministries: "Like good stewards of the manifold grace of God, serve one another with whatever gift each of you has received. Whoever speaks [ministry of the word] must do so as one speaking the very words of God; whoever serves [ministry of helping] must do so with the strength that God supplies" (1 Pet 4:10-11a). Various passages also indicate ministries of administration. One of the most notable of these passages relates to the appointment of the seven to supervise food distribution in the Jerusalem church (Acts 6:1ff.). However they may be named, churches have always needed and continue to need these types of ministry: proclamation, administration, and helping.

We also know what it means to be a good minister in any context and in any century, which is what we really need to know. Whatever they may be called, there are ministers today—bishops, elders, monks, pastors, teachers, deacons, etc.—who are good ministers, genuine servants of Christ in the service of his churches and humanity. There are also many in each category who are not good ministers when measured by the criteria laid down by Jesus himself. What matters is not so much the denominational context of their ministry, the title they have been given, or how that ministry is defined. Rather, what matters is how they measure up to the standards of ministry defined and lived by the Lord of the church. From this perspective, *there have been good and bad ministers* in every generation during the two millennia of Christian history.

THE APOSTOLIC MINISTRY

In our consideration of the early churches' ministry, we shall start with the apostolic ministry. Paul lists it first as the most important of the ministries of the word (1 Cor 12:28). In Ephesians 2:20 we read the assertion that the church is "built upon the foundation of the apostles and prophets."[2] We raise the question: Why did Paul consider the apostolic ministry the most important?

Although the Twelve were called apostles, let it be noted first of all that the term is not limited to them. The term means "messenger" or "one who is sent" and can be used broadly. However, when we talk about the apostolic ministry in the church, we understand that the term is used specifically. One clue to the more restricted meaning is found in the Acts passage that describes the selection of a person to replace Judas. The limitation is clear. The newest member of the Twelve was to be one of the people who had been with Jesus from the time of the baptism by John until the ascension. This was necessary if he was to be, as were the remaining eleven, "a witness . . . to his resurrection" (Acts 1:22).

Paul considered himself qualified to be an apostle, although many Jewish Christians evidently disputed his claim because he failed to meet the criteria, not having been with Jesus during his life. Nevertheless, he believed that his experience put him in the same category as the other apostles. In 1 Corinthians 9:1 he asks, "Am I not an apostle? Have I not seen Jesus our Lord?" This implies that the appearance of Jesus to him was on the same level as the appearances to the earlier apostles. Paul claimed that the risen Lord commissioned him directly, just as Jesus commissioned earlier apostles during his time on earth. Therefore, Paul was qualified to be a witness to the resurrected one (see Gal 1:11ff. and 1 Cor 9:1 for his defense of his apostleship). Paul knew that Jesus was alive because the Lord had appeared to him after his death.

Later in the same letter, Paul attested to the fact of Jesus' resurrection by listing the people to whom he had appeared after the crucifixion. He then concluded the list with these words, "Last of all, as to one untimely born, he appeared also to me. For I am the least of the *apostles*, unfit to be called an apostle . . ."(1 Cor 15:8-9a). Notice that Paul understood that the ministry of the apostle was to witness to the resurrection as a result of having seen Jesus alive after his crucifixion. Notice further that Paul claimed Jesus' encounter with him concluded the resurrection appearances.

How did he understand the difference between his status and that of Timothy or Luke, for example? Possibly the answer is that their conviction that Jesus was alive was mediated through the church and did not come as a result of a resurrection appearance. They became Christians through the hearing of the word. Others, however, had seen Jesus alive after his crucifixion, and their witness to that led to the faith of those who came after them. Paul placed himself in that group, although many others evidently rejected his claim.

This discussion shows why the apostolic ministry must be listed first. It was absolutely essential to the beginning of the church. Because the incarnation was an event, the only way people could learn about it was through the witness of those who had been with Jesus and to whom he had appeared after his death. If no one had been qualified and willing to tell the story, the influence of Jesus would have ended with his death. The apostolic ministry is the bridge between Jesus and subsequent generations. Apostles were not more important nor were they necessarily any more devoted than other believers, but their ministry was the most crucial for the beginning of the Christian community.

A MODERN APOSTOLIC MINISTRY?

This leads us to one of the great divisions among churches. Some Christians claim that a continuing apostolic ministry is essential to the authenticity of the church. The modern apostolic ministry of their church is carried on by bishops whose ordination goes back in an unbroken line to the first apostles. Among them are groups like the Roman Catholic Church, the Greek Orthodox church, and the Anglican church. From their perspective, churches without a continuing, contemporary apostolic ministry are not authentic churches. Such churches require that those who propose to join them from evangelical ranks be confirmed—that is, have *apostolic* hands laid on them.

Of course, the Roman Catholic Church goes even further in its assertion of the primacy of the bishop of Rome, who has a special authority over the whole of Christendom. The claim is that Peter received authority from Jesus (Matt 16:18-19), that he was the first bishop of Rome, and that his successors are to exercise his authority.

In this day of increased ecumenical interest, the primacy of the bishop of Rome is one of the great deterrents to the union of certain groups with the Roman Catholic Church.

There are serious problems regarding the Roman Catholic claims in terms of both the New Testament and history. The New Testament does not support the conception that the ministry of the apostles was understood as a continuing ministry in the history of the church. In this connection, refer to the quotation from 1 Corinthians above. Paul essentially drew a line beneath his apostolic ministry. He was the last of the apostolic witnesses. Also, in Acts 1:22, the role of the Twelve was to be witnesses qualified by their association with Jesus during his ministry and after his resurrection, which excludes those whose Christian faith is mediated through the apostolic witness. Also, in 1 Corinthians 14 Paul contrasted prophecy with tongues, asserting that prophecy was the gift the church should seek. The reason is that the prophetic gift was the most important gift available to the Corinthians. The apostolic gift was not a possibility and for that reason, therefore, was not mentioned. The Corinthian church could not receive that gift. Furthermore, in Romans 12:6, and for the same reason, Paul placed prophecy first as the most important gift available to the Roman believers.

Another related issue is the primacy of Peter among the apostles and his relationship with the Church at Rome. Tradition tells us that both Peter and Paul were martyred in Rome. Possibly that is true, although it cannot be proven. On the other hand, the evidence for Peter being the founder of the church in Rome is questionable. The most telling argument against it is the Epistle to the Romans. One can hardly believe that Paul would have written such a long letter to the church without ever once mentioning Peter's name if he had indeed been its bishop.

The ministry performed by the apostles in the first century does continue today, not in the form of living people, but in a collection of books we call the New Testament. The New Testament contains the apostolic witness, and it functions to keep alive the memory of who Jesus was, what he said, and what he did. The most important aspect of that witness, of course, is the apostles' testimony to the resurrection based on the appearances of the risen Lord to them. Thus, the New Testament is a central book in the life of the church. It does what no other book can do, no matter how inspired or helpful. It bridges the gap of the centuries and makes the event of the first century contemporary to us today. It keeps alive the memory of Jesus' life, death, and resurrection.

THE PROPHET

The second most important ministry in the New Testament is that of prophet. We have already noted the importance of the prophet in the Old Testament. The prophet was a minister who from time to time was especially endowed by the Spirit to receive and communicate the contemporary word of the Lord to God's often rebellious and stubborn people. The ministries of priest and Levite were necessary for the perpetuation of the liturgy in the temple. However, the prophets delivered God's contemporary message. Moses was considered one of the greatest prophets in Jewish religion. Therefore, according to their belief, the Law, the ultimate in God's revelation, was given through a prophet. There was also the belief in Jesus' day that God had not spoken directly to the people since the last of the prophets some 400 years before. However, an expectation of Jewish eschatalogical thought was that the gift of prophecy would be renewed with the coming of Messiah and the end of the age. As we have seen in the chapter on Pentecost, the Spirit would be poured out on all God's people, leaving as evidence the people's ability to prophesy (Acts 2:17).

Since all believers possess the Spirit, any one of them is capable of receiving the prophetic gift, i.e., of discerning the will of God in a given situation and proclaiming God's word to God's people. For the most part, churches have narrowed that concept and act as though only certain ministers, pastors or bishops for example, can proclaim God's contemporary message to the believing community. The truth, nevertheless, is that the pastor is no more qualified to fill the role of prophet than any member of the flock, for all have the same Spirit.

Paul believed that the prophetic gift was the most important one accessible to believers after his time. This is clear from a reading of 1 Corinthians 14 where Paul urges the Corinthians to seek to prophesy above all else. This does not mean that each individual should seek it as a special gift, but that the church needs to hear God's word for the moment through one or more of the members. When Paul listed the gifts by order of their importance, he placed prophecy second only to the apostolic gift (1 Cor 12:28).

Why did he place such an emphasis on the prophetic gift? The answer is that the church lives by the word of God. It cannot project, it cannot act, it cannot make decisions without a revelation from the Lord. In dealing with many important questions, of course, the church has the New Testament. But in every age there are questions to face, decisions to make, and actions to take for which there is no more than general guidance in the church's book. That has never been more true than in our time, with scientific discoveries and new possibilities that no one in the first century could have anticipated. If the church is going to continue to do the will of her Lord, it must continue to receive messages from the Lord through the Spirit of prophecy.

In facing the difficult problems of modernity, we must listen carefully to all kinds of people—teachers, pastors, church leaders however named, church members. Through any or all of them God can speak to churches. The question always arises: Do God's people exercise the gift of discernment (see 1 Cor 14:29) so that they recognize the word of God when they hear it? Paul believed that all Christians were able to determine whether they should say "Amen" to the message of the prophet because they also had the gift of the Spirit. Sadly, the darkest days and greatest failures of the churches throughout history have resulted from the failure of people—through prejudice, selfishness, or fear—to heed the prophetic voices of their day. In my opinion this was true of the Roman Catholic Church during the days leading up to the Reformation. It was also true of Protestant churches in the South during the time of the civil rights movement.

CHURCH LEADERS: ELDERS

It was almost inevitable that elders would be understood as a category of leadership in the early church. The Hebrew term came from a word that meant "beard" and therefore referred to a grown man, someone with a beard. Generally, the term applied to prominent people whose word and counsel commanded respect. The term was evidently used throughout the history of Israel to refer to individuals or groups who exercised leadership and authority in various ways in the life of the people. In the Judaism contemporary with the New Testament, every Jewish community had a governing council of elders. The most important of these councils was the Sanhedrin, often referred to in terms of its components, i.e., elders, chief priests, and teachers of the law (or scribes).[3]

It is not surprising, therefore, that the term elder was used in Jewish Christian communities to refer to church leaders. Although we are not told how the function of elders began, they appear without prelude in Acts 11:30. Of passing interest is the fact that the offering raised by the church at Antioch was sent to elders and not to apostles. Thereafter, elders are mentioned in various places in the book of Acts. It is clear from the passages that they exercised an important role in the decision-making processes of Christians gathered in Jerusalem (Acts 15:2, 4, 6, 22, 23).

We are also told that Paul appointed elders for each church, but no description is given of their duties (Acts 14:23). Note that the account does not indicate that the church had a role in the choice of the elders. Likewise, we are not told anything about the process by which Paul and Barnabas reached their decision. Clearly elders were to be leaders of the churches. Was their responsibility limited to administrative duties, or did it involve preaching? From the references we can infer that a number of elders served a given church, but that does not help us define their role. Titus is also instructed to "appoint elders in every town" (see Titus 1:5). These two passages would indicate that neither the author of Acts nor the writer of Titus believed the church necessarily had a voice in the appointments. However, the references are brief.

In 1 Peter the author uses the term "apostle" to refer to himself (1:1) and "elder" to refer to leaders of the church (5:1ff.). The Greek word translated "elder" can also mean an older person, and in this passage that meaning of the term comes into play. The younger people are instructed to accept the authority of the elders (5:5). This indicates that in the churches to which the epistle is directed, elders were older members of the church. No indication is given about the criteria for the office or the methodology for choosing the candidates. No specific clarification of their role is found in the epistle other than that they were leaders who should be respected.

One other important point should be noted. In most of the books of the New Testament the office of elder is not mentioned at all. The office is mentioned in Acts, 1 Timothy, Titus, James, and 1 Peter, the majority in Acts.[4]

CHURCH LEADERS: BISHOPS

Another category of church leaders found in the New Testament is that of bishop. We need to give attention to the basic meaning of the word, which indicates something of the bishop's ministry, at least in the earliest days of Christianity. Perhaps the most instructive text in the New Testament to help us understand the meaning of *episkopos* (bishop) is Matthew 25:36, where the cognate verb is used: "I was sick and you visited me" (see also Jas 1:27). But "to visit" means more than "to go see," the meaning generally associated with it in English. Visiting arises out of concern for the welfare of the person and has the purpose of helping in a situation of need. The word used in the text indicates that a person who cares undertakes the visit. In 1 Peter 2:25 Christ is called the "shepherd and bishop[5] of your souls." In this passage shepherd and bishop are synonymous terms.

This furnishes the background for the rise of the term to designate church leaders or officials. It should be noted that the New Testament use of bishop to designate a church leader is rare. This tells us that the office only became extremely important in post-apostolic days or, better, that the term used to designate the office was not popular in New Testament times. As reported in the book of Acts, Paul used the word (Acts 20:28) in addressing the elders of Ephesus, making elder and bishop synonymous in that context. [6] In his introduction to Philippians Paul sent greetings to the "saints" along with deacons and bishops. Does this indicate that there were two groups of officials in the church or simply that the functions could be filled at a given time by any members of the church? In any case, it is interesting that two or more people in the church could be addressed as bishop. The real development and definition of the office of bishop in the churches occurred primarily after the books of the New Testament were written.

The difficult and chaotic conditions that apparently arose in the later apostolic period and developed in the second century influenced the development of the office of bishop. Times called for strong and structured leadership exercised by people who could speak with an authoritative voice in the midst of so many divergent and conflicting voices. The bishop then became the office of authority to resolve conflicts, to define doctrine, and to determine the direction of the churches. This authority became focused early in the councils where bishops dealt with major disputes. Let it be noted that this process saved what we know as classical orthodox Christianity and prevented Gnosticism and other forces from fragmenting the Christian community. However much those of us who belong to the free church tradition may reject the structured approach of other churches, we need to acknowledge our indebtedness to those who defined the major tenets of our faith in very difficult times.

CHURCH LEADERS: PASTOR

Pastor (literally, shepherd) is used only once in the New Testament to signify church leaders (Eph 4:11). In this passage "teacher" is used apparently as an expansion on the role of the pastor. That is, pastor and teacher seem to refer to the same person. Since the term "pastor" is found only in the one place, it seems sound to conclude that it was not at that time an established title. Although the word was not used as a designation for church leaders, there is a great deal of material that serves as the basis for its later widespread use.

As we know pastor is an important term to describe the ministry of Jesus. He is the quintessential Shepherd of God's flock. He is the Messianic Shepherd of Jewish expectation, the one who had appeared to gather God's scattered flock (cf. Matt 15:24). Of course, the figure is also important in John's presentation of Jesus. He is the Good Shepherd. Conversely, the people of God are his sheep, in their totality, his flock. It is always appropriate to see the responsibility of church leaders, whatever they may be called, as that of a shepherd. A shepherd cares for the sheep, their welfare always of utmost importance, no sacrifice too great to make for them. The attitude of the shepherd is the complete opposite of demagogues who have exploited God's sheep through the centuries.

In my opinion, no title for the servant-leader of a church is more appropriate than that of pastor. It identifies the person with Jesus and defines the role that all of us should aspire to and that we fail, at least to some extent, to attain. Furthermore, if there is an aspect of the ministry for which the pastor should be better prepared, at least technically, than other members of the congregation, it is that of teacher. We could never qualify to be pastors of churches if we were required to be better morally or closer to God than all the members of the flock. I have found in every church of my acquaintance that some believers were superior to me in those areas. Nevertheless, I am, or should be, better equipped to be the teacher of the church than most of them would be. That is due to the fact that I have had the privilege of spending more time in preparation than they, learning about the history, languages, and ideas that serve as a background for the interpretation of the Bible.

CHURCH LEADERS: DEACONS

We have already noted that ministry in the New Testament can be divided into broad categories: ministry of the word, ministry of helping (*diakonia*), and administration, to name three. These always have been and still are essential ministries for the churches, whatever title is given to the people who perform them. The word, originally broad in its scope, that designated the helper or servant (*diaconos*) later became applied to one specific group of ministers. Our English word, deacon, is a transliteration of the Greek term. We use that term to designate an official position in Christian ministry. Although the title deacon has been widely used in Christian churches through the centuries, the interpretation of the function of deacon varies decidedly from church to church.

The appointment of the seven in Acts 6:1ff. is understood by many to be the beginning point of the office of deacon in the Christian community. This, however, is far from clear. The work that the seven were chosen to do was indeed a helping ministry. However, the information Acts gives about the ministry of Philip and Stephen, for example, shows them functioning as evangelists, as preachers, as witnesses. The description of their role in the early church is certainly different from the description of deacon in the average church today.

In Romans 16:1 Paul describes Phoebe as a deacon of the church. Also, in Philippians 1:1 he addresses the church and in addition the bishops and deacons. This is the only epistle of the widely recognized Pauline writings in which such an address is found. Was he talking about deacon as an official role in the church, or was he talking about function, i.e., the kind of service the deacons (helpers) rendered?

Only in the Pastorals can we find evidence that the office of deacon had become an official position. According to these texts, those chosen as deacons should exhibit many of the same qualities expected of bishops (1 Tim 3:8ff.). Nevertheless, the role that deacons played in the churches is not described. Attention is directed solely to their character. Thus, we are left in the dark if we want to design the role of the modern office of deacon in New Testament terms.

The statement by M. H. Shepherd is appropriate as we look back on our study to this point:

> The most difficult problem in the history of the development of the Christian ministry has to do with the transition from the varied

> ministries of the apostolic age to the three-fold orders of bishops, elders (or presbyters), and deacons that were universally established and recognized in the church by the time of Ignatius and Polycarp (ca. A.D. 120). The principal questions debated are: (a) the relation of bishops and elders—whether they were originally the same, and if not, how they were distinguished from one another; (b) the emergence of a single, monarchical bishop as the head of each Christian community; and (c) the means of the selection and ordination of these orders.[7]

Again we are driven to the conclusion that no modern church's organization would be recognizable to Christians of the first generation.

CHARISMATIC MINISTRIES

One of the issues often discussed by New Testament scholars today is the relationship between the more official understanding of ministry found in Acts and the Pastorals and the charismatic understanding we find in 1 Corinthians (especially chapters 12–14) and Romans 13. They wonder whether the role of the minister is defined by the church and if the decision of who should serve in that capacity is also made by the church. Is the ministry of the members determined by the members themselves as they respond to the inspiration of the Spirit in their lives? In other words, is a ministry an office or a function? Are ministers called to do a certain ministry, for example, prophecy, all their lives? Or does one's gift at a given moment depend on the moving of God's Spirit in the person's life at that particular moment?

Once again, the fact that the questions arise is due to the variety of texts we use in our attempt to understand ministry in the New Testament. It seems to me that we could well conclude that ministers in the Jerusalem church, as pictured in the book of Acts, were regarded as officials of the church. This would be a logical result of the influence of Judaism on the first Christian community. Elders had played a continuing role in various aspects of Hebrew and Jewish history, so it would be natural to think of the elders as an official council charged with governing the community. True, the congregation is brought into play to a certain extent. For example, the people played a role in the choice of a person to fill the vacant place among the Twelve (Acts 1:23). Nonetheless, their input was clearly limited and within the guidelines set by the leaders. In the choice of the seven to assist the apostles (Acts 6:1-6), the congregation played a significant role, but the apostles once again set the parameters. The decision to choose a committee, the number to comprise it, and the method of decision were spelled out clearly by the leaders.

In 1 Timothy elders or bishops and deacons are described in such a way that we conclude these leaders are understood as officials in the churches. Also, Timothy and Titus both exercise the authority of bishop in their geographical area, although that word is not used. There is a genuine contrast between the concept of ministry in the Pastorals and that found in 1 Corinthians. This kind of problem has caused most scholars to conclude that a disciple of Paul rather than Paul himself was the real author of the Pastorals.

By way of contrast to the Pastoral Epistles, in 1 Corinthians there is no indication that Paul could call on anyone vested with official authority to accept his instruction and deal with the problems in the church. The approach to making decisions was evidently congregational.[8] With a person of recognized official authority to tell the church what to do, it could not have gotten into the difficulties that plagued it. The Corinthian church seems to illustrate absolute freedom being abused absolutely. The Epistle to the Philippians was addressed to the church and to bishops and deacons. However, when Paul dealt with problems in the church, he did not appear to invoke an official authority to assure his requests were respected. He appealed to Euodia and Syntyche to resolve their conflict themselves (Phil 4:2). It is true that he called on an unnamed person he called "true yokefellow" to help the women, but the appeal does not indicate that the person had official authority. Surely in Galatians Paul would have indicated the option of calling on local officials to help him resolve problems in the churches—if that were possible. There is certainly no letter in which Paul reveals more frustration and unhappiness with a church. Throughout the letter, however, it seems that he appealed to the church to respond to his exhortations.

MINISTRY IN THE BAPTIST CONTEXT

We Baptists, along with a number of other denominations, opt for two major categories of official ministry in our churches, i.e., pastor and deacon. We justify this by understanding that bishop, elder, and pastor are synonymous terms, referring to the same office or function. Some texts offer evidence that this was true in New Testament churches. In Acts 20:17ff., for example, the three terms are used as apparent synonyms. The leaders are called elders (v. 17), and their work is described as that of overseers (bishops) in 20:28. Also, their task is to "care for" or "shepherd" (be pastors of) the flock.

The author of 1 Timothy apparently made no distinction between bishops and elders (compare 3:1-7 with 5:17-22). Incidentally, you will notice in 1 Timothy 5:17 that the task of the elder *could be* preacher and teacher, but the clear implication is that it did not have to include those functions. What did elders do who neither preached nor taught? We have no way of knowing. From these documents, we can assume that the bishops or elders played key roles in church leadership. How that leadership is to be defined, limited, or implemented in a given situation, however, is not at all clear. In my opinion, we cannot conclude that the role of church leaders, variously called bishops, elders, and perhaps pastors, was everywhere defined in the same way, nor can we know the possible limits different congregations imposed on their leadership.

Furthermore, Baptists and most other Protestant churches have one pastor, sometimes aided by a number of associates. In churches with multiple pastors, the leading pastor is given the title of senior pastor or minister. As with much of our vocabulary about ministry, this is not a New Testament label. As far as I can tell, the material in the New Testament gives us no reason to assume that individual churches had only one bishop or elder. Acts indicates that there were multiple leaders in the church in Jerusalem, whether apostolic leaders or elders. And elders certainly did not function in the same way as pastors in modern churches. Paul used the plural "bishops" in his address to the church at Philippi (Phil 1:1), thus indicating that there was more than one bishop in the church. We cannot know what the categories of ministers deemed desirable in each church in all places. However (and I repeat), one certainty is that no church in the New Testament was organized like any church in existence today. We can also conclude, I believe, that churches in different areas in New Testament times were organized differently, and ministers functioned differently in different places. We have only to compare the picture of the church in Jerusalem as described by Acts with what Paul's correspondence indicates about the church in Corinth.

CHURCH GOVERNMENT

The issue of the governance of the church is closely connected to the issue of ministry. Authority given by the church to the ministers determines the kind of governance. There are three kinds of church government in mainline churches: (1) episcopal, which emphasizes the authority of the bishop (*episkopos*), (2) presbyterian, in which authority is vested in the presbytery made up of elders and ministers, and (3) congregational, which emphasizes the decision-making role of the congregation.

The problem is that all three types have textual support in the New Testament. In Acts, the center of authority in Jerusalem is first composed of the apostles and the elders. One can suppose that the elder in Judaism had a great influence on the organization of the Christian community in that city. At any rate, the far-reaching decision about the terms for admitting Gentiles into the Christian fellowship (Acts 15:1ff.) was reached by the church under the leadership of the two groups, the apostles and the elders. Later James, brother of the Lord but not a member of the original group of disciples, is portrayed as the dominant leader of the Jerusalem church (Acts 21:18). How did that change take place and what does it say about a struggle for leadership in the Jerusalem church? These questions must be placed in the long list of those for which there is no clear answer. According to Acts, at the conclusion of their first so-called missionary journey, Paul and Barnabas appointed elders in every church (Acts 14:23). A survey of Acts, therefore, assigns a limited role to the congregations in the decisions that were made.

The same general picture is evident in the Pastorals. In the letter addressed to Titus, the writer gives Titus the authority to appoint the elders in the churches. The role of monarchical bishop, at least in embryonic form, can be justified from the Pastorals. The qualifications for bishops and deacons are outlined for Timothy, according to the first letter that bears his name (1 Tim 3:1ff.), rather than given to churches. This could mean that Timothy was responsible for choosing these officials. We see, therefore, that vesting authority in the bishop or in elders can be supported well by various New Testament texts.

What about the congregational approach? I think the strongest argument for this system of church governance is found in Paul's major and undisputed epistles—Galatians, 1 and 2 Corinthians, and Romans. Paul addressed none of his major letters to church authorities, in contrast to the Pastorals that are addressed to authority figures. In every case he addressed the church. It is difficult to believe that he would not have referred to the bishop or governing officers of the church if such existed. As it was, he apparently left it up to the church to solve its problems. A good example is 1 Corinthians 5 where Paul deals with a serious problem. A man was living with his father's wife. Evidently, he flaunted it, and the church was little concerned about this serious moral problem. What did Paul do? He called on the church when it was next assembled (1 Cor 5:4) to address the matter, leaving no doubt about what he thought the church ought to do. However, he apparently was unsure that the church would accept his directions as authoritative. In the final analysis, the congregation itself would be responsible for the decision. Again, the mechanism by which the decision would be made is unknown to us.

A congregational approach to decision-making is also congenial with the doctrine of the priesthood of every believer to which Baptists and others subscribe. The doctrine means that there is no official of the church with any more access to God than its most humble member. It means that a church member can discern what God wants for the church just as much as the pastor or any other official or group of officials can.

Baptists often talk about the governance of the church in political terms. It is often said that a Baptist church is a democracy. The concept that all members have equal rights and privileges is drawn from this political definition. Both ideas are wrong from the New Testament point of view. The church is not a democracy. It is a people under the lordship of Christ who are called to do the will of the Lord. The correct approach is to understand that the participation of members in decision-making is not theirs by right, belonging to them because the church is a democracy. Each member has the capacity to participate in the process because he or she has been endowed with the Spirit. Their "vote" on an issue should represent their response to the leadership of the Spirit in that particular matter. To participate in the decision-making of the Lord's church is not a right; rather, it is an awesome responsibility.

Another pernicious idea persists that has been the cause of schisms in many churches. I refer to the idea that churches, like democratic institutions, decide on actions on the basis of a majority vote. That is, a vote of 50 percent plus one carries the day. Such an idea is totally contrary to the concept of the priesthood of all believers. It also ignores the biblical record, which shows that the minority in many such cases is often the group that understood the will of God correctly. The only approach in accord with the idea that every member is capable of discerning the leadership of the Spirit is *consensus*. Wise leaders have always operated on this principle, often for practical reasons rather than because of theological perspective. Many leaders, nevertheless, often lack the patience to wait for consensus to develop. Often we are obsessed with completing the project rather than concerned with the development of the congregation into a people who love God and love one another. All of us have known of churches that implemented a decision based on a slim majority only to split the congregation asunder.

FINANCIAL SUPPORT OF MINISTERS

There is another issue related to ministry that, in my experience, is not always addressed from a New Testament or theological perspective. It is the question of the financial support of ministers. Anybody well acquainted with the New Testament is aware of textual underpinning for such support. According to Luke 10:7, Jesus instructed his disciples, whom he was sending on a mission, to depend on the people of the towns they would visit for their support. This verse contains the dictum "the laborer deserves to be paid." The Apostle Paul gave unqualified support to this practice in 1 Corinthians 9:3-24 where we find this statement: "the Lord commanded that those who proclaim the gospel should get their living by the gospel" (9:14). In spite of the conviction that he was within his right to receive material compensation for his labors, Paul decided that he would earn his living own while in Corinth (1 Cor 9:15). Also, in 1 Timothy 5:18 we read "for the scripture says, 'You shall not muzzle an ox while it is treading out the grain,' and, 'The laborer deserves to be paid.'"

From the citations above we can see that there is widespread textual foundation for the material support of ministers. We can also assume that, at least in the majority of the cases, the support related to basic needs. Especially in the case of the itinerant preachers who were a factor in the spread of Christianity, food and shelter would have been basic requirements. Hospitable Christians in the areas visited could provide such support.

It is also clear that the material needs of people in the first century, when the vast majority always lived right on the edge economically, differ greatly from the needs of people in our day. That is especially true in a modern industrialized country. For example, we would assume that providing for the education of our children is a basic need. In our society, therefore, ministers should receive enough financial support to be able to pay for their children's education.

AMOUNT OF FINANCIAL SUPPORT

Practical aspects of this issue faced by churches today are not clearly treated in the texts. The first question addresses the amount of support provided for ministers in any given church. This is certainly a question that Protestant churches face over and over again. Many times they resolve it by surveying their sister churches, intending not to be the church with the lowest compensation in the geographic area. In order to help the churches resolve the question, denominations often publish information that gives a picture of the varying levels of support in the churches affiliated with them.

Some texts relate to this issue. One is 1 Timothy 5:17: "Let elders who rule well be considered worthy of double honor, especially those who labor in preaching and teaching." Although the word translated "honor" may mean exactly that, it is probably used here for compensation. The new idea introduced in this text is the author's opinion that diligence and competence should be recognized and rewarded financially.

Two texts in the Pauline epistles illuminate this matter of material support for ministers. In Philippians 4:15 Paul says, "You Philippians indeed know that in the early days of the gospel, when I left Macedonia, no church shared with me in the matter of giving and receiving, except you alone."[9] In Galatians 6:6 we read: "Those who are taught the word must share in all good things with their teacher." Paul uses the same verb in each of these two verses. Translated as "share with" in both texts, it means "to have fellowship with." This is a good translation in those cases.

The basic theological concept underlying the idea is that all of us as believers are members of the same family or community. All members of the community bring what they have to contribute to the community, and all members receive from the community what they need. In the verses cited above, some contribute ministry in the form of the communication or teaching of the gospel, and others provide the material support.

Now we turn back to the question at hand. What should be the amount of the support? The answer is determined by how the congregation interprets what it means to share. A church whose members receive an average income of twenty thousand dollars per year would obviously interpret the meaning of sharing differently from a church whose members' annual income averages seventy thousand dollars. From my point of view, a logical answer is that the minister's support should approximately match the average income of the congregation. From this perspective, surveys of other churches in the area are more or less irrelevant. Of greatest importance is the individual church's decision about what it means for that particular church to share.

Our discussion is applicable when the local church determines the income of the minister. A somewhat different approach would be used when the denomination has a role in setting the amount. However, the question is still the same: What does it mean to share in a particular context?

CHOOSING WHICH MINISTERS TO SUPPORT

Another related question for which the New Testament gives no clear example or teaching relates to the selection of ministers who receive support. One of the primary developments in modern ecclesiology is the belief, based on Paul's writings especially to the Corinthians and Romans, that every believer is a minister. All have gifts that equip them to minister, and no one member is more responsible for fulfilling that ministry than any other. I grew up hearing the phrase "full-time minister" to describe ministers, such as pastors, who were supported financially by the churches. As many of us have realized, the phrase is inappropriate in that context because, rightly understood, all believers are called to live out their ministry all of the time. All Christians are called to be "full-time ministers."

There is another modern development that further complicates the issue. In my early childhood, the only ordained ministers in most Baptist churches were pastors. A few of the more affluent churches had assistant ministers, primarily in the areas of education and music. That has changed drastically in more recent times. Even small churches may have two or three so-called "staff ministers."[10] This means that churches have multiple ministers whom they support financially.

Now we turn back to the question: How do you decide to support one minister and not others? My answer would be that support depends upon what is demanded of a particular minister. If churches want ministers who dedicate their efforts to the work of the church to the extent that earning a living otherwise is impossible, the church members need to share what they earn with them. Churches often have members who *voluntarily* give about as much time to the work of the church as the paid ministers do. However, they are not dependent on the church for support and are not required by the church to perform their ministry. Such ministers do not expect, do not need, and should not receive material support for what they do.

NOTES

[1] Bishop Stephen Neil said in a sermon preached in our seminary, "If you are not willing to spend the rest of your life serving a small church in Appalachia, you are not worthy of being a Christian minister."

[2] Many scholars believe that Ephesians was written by an admirer of Paul and not by the apostle himself, a common practice in that time. However, there are good scholars who defend the traditional view.

[3] See, for example, Mark 14:43 and similar references.

[4] Most scholars have concluded that the references to the appointment of elders by a superior relate to a somewhat later time. Early on, the chaotic conditions related to the rise of Gnosticism caused the churches to tighten their procedures and seek to put in place authoritative church leaders who could make decisions to deal with the conditions.

[5] "Guardian" in the NRSV.

[6] Translated "overseer" in the NRSV.

[7] M. H. Shepherd Jr., "Ministry, Christian" *The Interpreter's Dictionary of the Bible*, vol. 3, ed. George Arthur Buttrick et al. (New York: Abingdon Press, 1962), 389.

[8] See for example what Paul wrote to the Corinthian church about what he viewed as a serious problem the church needed to address. He called on the church to make the decision when it assembled (5:4), making it fairly clear that it was the responsibility of the congregation to do so. There is no hint about the nature of the decision-making process.

[9] This verse shows that Paul was not averse to receiving support for himself, although for his own reasons he spurned it in Corinth.

[10] Notice the different adjectives used to describe ministers that have no model in the New Testament. Paul had assistants, but he did not call them assistants. He used phrases like "fellow worker," "fellow soldier," "our brother." It seems to me that these are much more appropriate than modern terms derived from the corporate model.

Worship Elements

In a previous chapter, the importance of the church was discussed. A high involvement in the life of the church indicates that many people believe it is important. However, people are not always aware of what is most important about the church. I would say that proclaiming the gospel so that people can come to faith, building a community of faith and love, and ministering with compassion to the less fortunate are among the most important aspects of church life. Churches need to invest the energy of their members in these tasks.

However, essential to the missions of the church is the worship of the church. Assuming what we believe is true, the gathering together of God's people to praise God, proclaim their faith, hear a prophetic word from God, and receive instruction for their task is the most important assembly of people anywhere. Authentic worship energizes and provides direction for the life of the church. Also, assembling to worship God is one of the major ways that the church testifies to the reality of its faith in a world that does not know God. Believers gather to worship God because God deserves to be worshiped. Worship is the way they express their awe and wonder in the presence of the One who created them, continues to sustain them, and above all redeemed them, motivated only by an incredible love that we call grace. In this and the following two chapters, some of the elements important to the issue of worship are discussed.

JEWISH BACKGROUND

The first Christians did not have to create a liturgy—a program of worship for their assemblies—from scratch. They were reared in the Jewish traditions of worship, which revolved around religious activities of the synagogue, the temple, and the family. Before the end of the apostolic age, the temple in Jerusalem was destroyed by the Roman legions (AD 70) and was no longer available for worship. In Jesus' day it was the center of the Jewish sacrificial system. Many Jews, however, especially those living outside Palestine, never attended the temple during their lifetime. On the other hand, the quorum for a synagogue service was ten male Jews, which means that a synagogue could exist wherever ten Jewish men lived. Thus, the synagogue was the most significant institution in the lives of the great majority of Jews. It was the place where the Pharisees held sway and where the religious outlook and beliefs of the people were shaped.

The synagogue probably originated among captive Jews in Babylon. It became the vital institution for the preservation of Jewish life and traditions. It functioned as the community center for the Jewish population throughout the Roman Empire. No doubt, the synagogue played a central role in the preservation of Jewish institutions and religious life during times of exile and persecution. Of course, one crucial aspect of that life was the Sabbath service that took place weekly. We have a fairly clear idea about the various synagogue activities and about the structure of its worship when Christianity came into being.

The Shema, the Jewish confession of faith, was recited at the beginning of the service: "Hear, O Israel: The LORD is our God, the LORD alone. You shall love the LORD your God with all your heart, and with all your soul, and with all your might" (Deut 6:4-5). The Shema was followed by a prayer consisting of eighteen benedictions, so called because each one of them is introduced by the phrase "Blessed art thou, O Lord."

The reading of Scripture formed an important part of the service. In the first century, the Pentateuch reading evidently followed a fixed pattern that took the listeners through those books in three years. A reading from the prophets followed the Pentateuch reading. It is unclear whether the assigned reader chose this passage or one of the synagogue officers determined it. It was from these public readings in the synagogue that Jesus and his early followers became acquainted with the Hebrew Scriptures. A sermon or homily also figured in the service if a person deemed competent to deliver it was present. Often visitors were asked to deliver the sermon, which explains why Jesus was given this opportunity when visiting the synagogue in Nazareth (Luke 4:16ff). It is clear that the reading of Scripture, prayers, and the sermon were aspects of the synagogue service that carried over into Christian worship.

CHRISTIAN WORSHIP IN THE SECOND CENTURY

Our first clear outline of an early Christian worship service comes from the middle of the second century, more than one hundred years after the beginnings of Christianity. It is found in the writings of Justin Martyr and reflects the kind of service one would have encountered in a Roman church.[1] According to Justin, Sunday was the day the churches congregated for worship because Jesus was raised on the first day of the week. As he outlined the worship, it began with (1) a reading from the memoirs of the apostles[2] or the prophets followed by (2) instructions and exhortations, i.e., a sermon, delivered by the president. Following this (3) the congregation arose for prayers and at their conclusion said the amen. When the prayers ended, (4) bread, wine, and water were brought for the celebration of the Eucharist.[3] The president led in thanksgiving and prayers followed by the distribution of the elements to each member. (5) The deacons sent the elements to the homes of those who were absent so they could participate in the Supper. The last item mentioned is (6) an offering for the purpose of helping "the orphans and widows, and those who, through sickness or any other cause, are in want, and those who are in bonds, and the strangers sojourning among [them], and in a word take care of all who are in need."[4]

In addition, Justin gave notes about a service that included the ordinance of baptism.[5] The candidate was first taken to the place of baptism and after baptism was brought to the place where the congregation assembled.[6] The congregation offered prayers for the baptized, for themselves, and for others. Subsequently the members saluted each other with a holy kiss (cf. 1 Thess 5:26). Then they participated in the Eucharist or Lord's Supper in the way described above.

As time went on, the churches were more closely knit together administratively, and the pressure to conform became greater and greater. Consequently, I think we may conclude that at a fairly early date, many if not most of the churches of the Roman Empire conducted their services in a similar way. As we can see from modern practices, the worship services of most churches are not original but are similar to services in other churches.

Our problem is that we lack information needed to bridge the gap from the synagogue service to information about worship in the post-apostolic churches. For the hundred or so years prior to Justin Martyr, we do not have a detailed outline of worship in any of the communities mentioned in the New Testament. The account in Acts indicates that the earliest Jewish Christians continued to worship as a part of the larger Jewish community: "Day by day, as they spent much time together in the temple, they broke bread at home and ate their food with glad and generous hearts" (Acts 2:46). Of course, habitual worship in the temple was possible only to Christians in Jerusalem. Early on, two key factors in their worship that distinguished them from their Jewish environment are mentioned. They ate together and, according to Acts 2:41, they had conducted their first baptismal service. It appears that we can say with assurance that baptism and a meal were ubiquitous parts of Christian worship, whatever differences existed. From the beginning both of these were important parts of Christian worship.

The book of Acts tells us that Paul continued to go to synagogue services as long as this was open to him. One of the aspects of worship of which he evidently took advantage was the invitation often extended to someone present to deliver the homily. When he was invited to do this, he attempted to show the Jewish worshipers that Jesus was the long-awaited Messiah of their expectations—a message that was met with mixed reactions, as recorded in the Acts accounts.

The participation of Christians in Jewish worship in the synagogue ended by the close of the first century, as the gulf between church and synagogue widened. A major factor in this process was the growth of the gospel among non-Jews for whom the Jewish traditions were not important. For Jewish Christians, attending the services evidently became impossible after the adoption of the so-called 19th benediction in which the destruction of "Nazarenes and heretics," i.e., Christians, was called for. Possibly it was adopted to eliminate Christians' participation in synagogue worship. The synagogue, however, had already exerted its influence on Christian liturgy. What seems clear is that there is a line that begins in the synagogue and extends to Christian worship in the days of Justin Martyr and, indeed, to our day. Scripture reading, prayers, and the homily or sermon, all aspects of synagogue services, are important parts of most Christian services today. In addition, from the beginning Christian communities observed the two important ordinances or sacraments—the Lord's Supper and baptism.

VARIATION IN THE NEW TESTAMENT

The New Testament affords us an occasional glimpse into early church worship. From the text, we can conclude that there was a great deal of variety. This would have been inevitable. The churches were small and widely separated and could not maintain the kind of close contact possible in today's world. Furthermore, they were born in environments very different from one another.

The Jerusalem church depicted in the early part of Acts seems to have been a well-ordered community. For one thing, the church was led by apostles who enjoyed the respect of people who had come to faith as a result of their preaching. The apostles took the lead in making decisions. Church members seem to have been involved at least to some extent but in a manner dictated by the apostles (cf. Acts 6:1-6).

On the other end of the spectrum, in what could have been an extreme case, the worship of the Corinthian community apparently was characterized by chaos. One of Paul's major concerns in writing 1 Corinthians was to recommend a worship approach that would preserve the dynamic involvement of the Spirit and at the same time bring about a measure of order. Even if the church followed the admonitions given by the apostle in 1 Corinthians 14:26-33, the character of the service was probably vastly different from that in a community of Jewish Christians. Many of us, accustomed to an orderly, prearranged liturgy, would not feel at home in the kind of worship that evidently took place in Corinth. Such a service would be too free-flowing, too noisy, and too emotional for some of us.

Evidently there was no set order of worship for the Corinthian congregation to follow, unlike the service outlined by Justin Martyr above. Nobody waited to be invited to speak. People spoke, prayed, sang, etc. as they felt impelled by the Spirit and as long as they felt led to speak, often when with others speaking at the same time. Paul attempted through his instructions to get them to adopt an approach that would limit the number of people who spoke in any one service (1 Cor 14:26-33). He urged that only one person speak at a time and that no more than three speak in a service, suggesting that the person speaking cease to do so when another person felt led by the Spirit to speak. He anticipated objections from people who would say that they could not cease to speak so long as they were controlled by the Spirit. Paul's reply to that is interesting: "the spirits of prophets are subject to the prophets" (1 Cor 14:32). In other words, the speakers could cease speaking whenever they decided to do so, regardless of how strongly they felt gripped by the Spirit.

The Apostle enunciated two principles that should govern the church at worship: (1) Everything done in the service should contribute to the edification of the church, that is, the spiritual growth of everyone present (1 Cor 14:26). (2) The church was to be governed by the principle that God was not the author of chaos but of order (1 Cor 14:33; cf. Gen 1).

Admittedly, the worship of the Corinthian congregation and that of the Jerusalem church may have marked the two extremes of early church practice in worship. We may surmise, however, that worship inevitably varied to some extent from church to church and from culture to culture. Two aspects of early church worship, however, apparently existed everywhere, i.e., the Supper and baptism. At the same time, we see that a liturgy grounded in the synagogue experience of the first Christians and modified by the unique aspects of the Christian gospel eventually became standard for churches. With variations, that pattern can be seen in Christian worship today.

THE LORD'S SUPPER

As we have already noted, the Lord's Supper or Eucharist was an important part of the Christian worship from the beginning. We need to note, however, that it differed in an important way during the time of the New Testament. The reference that gives us the most information about the observance of the Supper in the early churches is found in 1 Corinthians 11:17ff. It is apparent that the Supper consisted of more than partaking of the loaf and drinking from the cup. From the comments made about it by the Apostle, one concludes that it was a banquet, not limited to the bread and wine as is commonplace today. Some members of the church gorged themselves and became drunk from the wine. Interestingly, the apostle did not castigate the Corinthians for their drunkenness. His main complaint about the way the Corinthians conducted the Supper was that they excluded the poorer members of the church from the feast. Probably these were slaves and others who were not at leisure to arrive at the place of meeting when the more affluent did.

In rebuking the erring members, Paul focused attention on the two elements of bread and wine. Thus he gave us the only account of the institution of the Supper by Jesus outside the Synoptic Gospels. He called attention to the seriousness of the action in which the erring members indulged. After all, as Jesus had said, the Supper was a memorial to him, a reminder of the death of the church's Lord. By selfishly partaking of the elements, they were "profaning the body and blood of the Lord (1 Cor 11:27), an extremely serious charge. "Discerning the body" in 11:29 is possibly a reference to the church as the body of Christ. Through the death of Christ, a people had been brought into being who were one in him. All were brothers and sisters; all of equal worth; all, especially the lowliest ones, were to be treated with love and respect. In excluding some members of the church, the erring members had partaken of the Supper "in an unworthy manner." They had introduced a schism into the body. By a callous disregard for other brothers and sisters, they had broken the "new covenant" by which they were bound together. This passage by Paul is the most elaborate theological treatment of the Supper in the New Testament.

A CONTINUATION OF THE FELLOWSHIP MEALS

In the New Testament, the celebration of the Lord's Supper includes a continuation of the fellowship meals that the disciples enjoyed together. In order to understand the importance of these meals, we need to know that eating together meant much more in the Semitic culture of Palestine than it does among us today. Meals often had a significant religious meaning, not only in Judaism but also in pagan religions, as expressions of fellowship between the people and their God. The meals were also expressions of fellowship between human beings. Thus, when Jesus announced he was going to Zacchaeus's house to eat (Luke 19:1ff.), everybody understood the meaning of that act. Zacchaeus also understood it and responded to the gesture. It meant that Jesus accepted Zacchaeus into his circle. In this light we can better understand the criticism of Jesus by his enemies: "This fellow welcomes sinners and eats with them" (Luke 15:2). Jesus' eating in the homes of people whom the Pharisees and others considered outside the pale meant that Jesus accepted them and identified with them. The parables that Jesus told in response to their criticism emphasize that in Jesus' act of fellowship God was also acting and receiving sinners. Instead of criticizing, therefore, the proper response was to join God in rejoicing. During his public ministry, Jesus ate with his disciples as an expression of his solidarity with them. After the incarnation, the early Christians continued eating together as a way of continuing their relationship with Jesus and with one another.

One meal in the ministry of Jesus took on a special importance and established a precedent for the disciples' meals in the future. During the Passover meal, a celebration of the most important event in the history of Israel, Jesus directed attention toward two elements of the meal, the breaking of bread at the beginning and the cup of wine at the end. Jesus gave thanks at the breaking of the bread, the common way for Jews to begin any meal. Thus, the Lord's Supper is often called the Eucharist, an anglicized version of the Greek word for "thanksgiving." Moreover, Jesus attached a new significance to the breaking of the bread. It represented his body. Every time the disciples participated in such a meal, they were to remember his death. The cup represented his blood and was to remind them that the giving of his life instituted a new covenant, i.e., a different basis for their relationship with God.

In the earliest days of Christian history, the meals of believers evidently combined both the Eucharist and the fellowship meals. As in the Passover where Jesus instituted it, the fellowship meal was possibly framed by the Eucharist (the two special elements of a banquet to which Jesus gave particular significance). In this light we can understand that the meals signified by the phrase "broke bread" (cf. Acts 2:46) were probably both the Lord's Supper and a fellowship meal.

Later political developments forced Christians to end the practice described above. A persecution occurred during the reign of the emperor Trajan (AD 98–117) when Christians were harassed for the crime of being Christian. Among other measures taken by Trajan, unlicensed clubs were forbidden to gather for meals. Christian churches were placed in this category. Faced by such circumstances, Christians separated the Eucharist, which was so important in their worship, from the meal itself. The name by which these fellowship meals were known is "Agape" or "love feasts." Thus, from the outline of Christian worship given by Justin Martyr we can see that the fellowship meal was not combined with the Lord's Supper at that point. It consisted of the two elements, the breaking of bread and the participation in the cup.

THE MEANING OF THE LORD'S SUPPER

Views about the nature and meaning of the Lord's Supper vary greatly and are one of the elements that divide different Christian groups. On one end of the spectrum is the emphasis on the bread and the wine as symbolic elements, representing the body and blood of Jesus. This is the position of Baptists, the group among whom I have lived and worked, and other evangelicals. In general they call baptism and the Lord's Supper ordinances and shy away from the word "sacrament." An ordinance is an authoritative decree. Thus, churches participate in the two ordinances because Christ commanded us to do so.

At the other extreme is the view of the Roman Catholic and Orthodox Churches. They teach that the elements are transformed in the miracle of the mass into the actual body and blood of Jesus. As such, it is an extremely important sacrament. Through it God's grace becomes effective in the daily life of the believer. The more devout participate in the Eucharist daily. Devoted members of the church celebrate the mass at least once a week. Between these two extremes are, for example, Lutheran and Anglican churches who teach that Christ is present alongside and linked to the elements in the Eucharist. With the consumption of the elements Christ enters into the life of the believer.

As is often the case, I find myself somewhere between various views. There is no doubt that the New Testament says Jesus commanded us to baptize and observe the Lord's Supper as the word ordinance emphasizes. In my opinion, however, as I stated in the chapter on baptism, symbol is an inadequate word for describing the Supper. It is indeed highly symbolic, as is baptism. However, the Supper is also a sacrament if one means by that word something through which God acts to administer grace and change lives. Through it, rightly understood and observed, it is possible for believers to enter into an intimate relationship with the Lord of the church and his people. The experience of relationship is much more than a symbol. It is, or can be, a life-changing moment in one's life. The kind of relationship possible through the Supper is an expression of the grace of God, of God's presence in and through our lives. Thus, from that point of view the Supper can also legitimately be called a sacrament.

The story found in Luke 24:13-27 probably illustrates this more than any other and possibly was included by Luke for that reason. At first, the two disciples did not recognize Jesus. Their lives were under the cloud of despair caused by the recent crucifixion of Jesus and the demise of their hopes and dreams. Only in their eating together did the disciples recognize they were in fellowship with Jesus. Eating with him marked the birth of a new hope and a great faith. For them that was truly a sacramental moment. God ministered to them through the meal. In many evangelical churches the experience of participating in the Supper does not seem to be a moment when people have a special experience of the presence of God. It also does not seem to be the moment when believers have an unusual sense of their intimate involvement with one another in the body of Christ. People have been taught to believe that it is "only" a symbol as a reaction against Roman Catholic theology.[7] It is true that symbols can be highly evocative. However, to think of something as "only" a symbol limits the capacity for understanding it as a possible profound spiritual experience. The challenge for those churches is to help people see the tremendous spiritual meaning possible in the moment when they break bread together before the table at which the Lord is host.

In 1 Corinthians 11:27 Paul wrote, "Whoever, therefore, eats the bread or drinks the cup of the Lord in an unworthy manner will be answerable for the body and blood of the Lord." My earliest memory of the wrong interpretation of the phrase "in an unworthy manner" goes back to my beloved grandmother. She told us about a man who would never participate in the Supper because he was sinful and, therefore, not worthy to partake of the elements. Understood that way, of course, most people would never participate. However, what Paul had in mind primarily was the relationship among the members of the Corinthian congregation. The way they partook of the Supper indicated that some of the members did not have a Christian understanding of their relationship with other members as brothers and sisters. From this point of view, to participate in the Supper without openness and love toward everyone who participates with us is to do so unworthily. Eucharist says that we come to the Lord's table with profound thanksgiving for all God has done for us through our Lord. It is a good term for the Supper. Communion—communion with the Lord who initiated the Supper and is present every time we celebrate it, and communion with those other members of the family united by faith in God through Jesus—is also a wonderful word for the observance in the light of what Paul wrote.

NOTES

[1] 1 Apology 65-67. Justin was a great apologist for Christianity to the Roman government in a time when Christians were under grave suspicion and, from the point of view of people like Justin, vastly misunderstood. Martyr is a sobriquet given to Justin because of his courageous martyrdom for his faith.

[2] These were the Gospels, of course. The use of these books in the liturgy of the churches tells us that they had been elevated to canonical status by this time.

[3] The water was mixed with the wine.

[4] 1 Apology 67.

[5] 1 Apology 65.

[6] This indicates that sprinkling or pouring were not used in the service. There would have been no need to go a place of baptism if a small amount of water had sufficed.

[7] Beliefs that are forged in reaction to another position are often warped. They are not arrived at in freedom.

Worship: Holy Places

If people assemble for worship, it goes without saying that they must congregate in a designated place. In most religions of the world, people generally regard as holy the places and buildings where they gather to worship or the places they associate with the presence of God. When they are in that place or near that place, they believe they are closer to the presence of their god than they would be in any other location. They make pilgrimages to the shrines. They bring their crippled and infirm there because they think a miracle is more possible in the holy place.

As all of us know, the Judaism in which the earliest followers of Jesus were nurtured had its sacred places. The land itself was a special area, the "Holy Land" as people often call it today. Within that land Jerusalem was a holy city that would become the center of a redeemed world according to the vision of the prophets. As Isaiah expressed it, "for the LORD of Hosts will reign on Mount Zion and in Jerusalem" (24:23). Jerusalem was the holiest city in the holy land, and the mount on which the temple was erected was the holiest area in that city. The concept of holiness intensified as one arrived at the temple complex[1] and moved toward the sanctuary, the holy place. The most sacred spot of all was the part of the building behind the curtain that divided the sanctuary. This was "the holiest place," or holy of holies as it is often called. In earlier days the ark of the covenant and the cherubim were found there. At this place, one was nearer to God than at any other location in the world.

The closer one got to the holiest place, the more restricted the entrance became. The only part of the temple complex accessible to Gentiles was the Court of the Gentiles. This area was defined by a balustrade with a sign warning Gentiles not to go beyond it. The women could go beyond the balustrade into the Court of the Women but no further. Israelite men could enter into the Court of Israel.

Only priests were allowed into the Court of Priests, the area immediately surrounding the sanctuary where the altar of sacrifice was found. Only they could enter the holy place, the first part of the sanctuary where the table of the presence, the incense altar, and the menorah were placed.[2] As said above, however, only the high priest could enter the holiest place and only once a year on the Day of Atonement. Once a year, as a part of a complex ceremony whose purpose was to atone for his sins and those of the people, the priest sprinkled blood on the mercy seat. Therefore, if Jews wanted to get close to God, they had to go to Jerusalem and go as far into the temple complex as they were allowed to go. In the final analysis, they had to depend on the high priest to represent them before God on the holiest day of the year in the holiest place of all. The people themselves were not able to approach the divine presence that closely.

THE NEW HOUSE OF WORSHIP

According to certain texts in the New Testament, the holy places described above were all changed radically. They were stripped of their meaning. There were to be no more holy spots in terms of geography or building. Anywhere in the world could be as holy as any other place. A significant statement is found in John's account of Jesus' conversation with the Samaritan woman. At some time in the past the Samaritans had split from the Jews (the Samaritan Schism) and had established their rival worship on Mount Gerizim, where their own priesthood ministered. In John 4:21 Jesus said, "Woman, believe me, the hour is coming when you will worship the Father neither on this mountain [Gerizim] nor in Jerusalem." He added in 4:23, "But the hour is coming, and is now here, when the true worshipers will worship the Father in spirit and truth, for the Father seeks such as these to worship him."

This was a revolutionary idea. It freed God from attachment to a place. One could get just as close to God anywhere in the world as one could on the temple mountain or in the holy building. Any place had the possibility of becoming the holiest place.[3] The most important truth we can derive from Jesus' declaration is that every person has an equal opportunity to draw near to God. God is available anywhere to anybody at any time! We do not need to approach God through some other human being or in some particular place. We call this the priesthood of the believer.

In the Acts account of his martyrdom, Stephen made a significant and relevant statement in his sermon to his accusers when he said, "Yet the Most High does not dwell in houses made with human hands" (7:48).[4] This would have been understood by his Jewish audience as undermining the importance of their temple as the house of God. Stephen's radical statement helped feed the flames of their rage that resulted in his stoning.

The Apostle Paul also made statements that affect the relationship of place to worship. In 1 Corinthians 3:16 he asked, "Do you not know that you are God's temple and that God's Spirit dwells in you?" Some important things are not clear in the English translation. First, the "you" is the second-person plural and refers to the church. Second, the word "temple" is a translation of a Greek word (*naos*) used to designate the sanctuary into which the people in general could not enter and where it was thought God's presence was nearest to the people. Therefore, the church assembled becomes a temple in which God dwells with all the possibilities that the presence of the Eternal implies. In 2 Corinthians 6:16 the apostle stated, "For we are the temple of the living God." He substantiated this by a quotation from Leviticus 26:12: "as God said, "I will live in them and walk among them, and I will be their God, and they shall be my people." In Romans 12:1 the individual Christian is pictured as a temple, a place where worship takes place. Therefore, anywhere God's people gather or a believer is found can be a holy place, a temple, because God is present there through the Spirit. This means that God dwells in God's people rather than in a shrine constructed by human hands. After all, the presence of God makes a place holy. Worship can take place anywhere the people of God find themselves. It can be by the bank of a river or in a cathedral.

Such statements mean Paul understood that there were no longer any sacred places as such, that God was not encountered in a sacred building, a house of God, but that God's presence was to be encountered in a special way in people. Other writers express the understanding that the people of God are the new temple, the house of God, and the place of the manifestation of the Spirit. In 1 Peter 2:4-5 we read, "Come to him, a living stone, though rejected by mortals yet chosen and precious in God's sight, and like living stones, let yourselves be built into a spiritual house, to be a holy priesthood, to offer spiritual sacrifices acceptable to God through Jesus Christ" (see also Eph 2:19-22).

THE REVERSAL

It was not long, however, before Christians began to attach special significance to places and to believe that God was more accessible in those places than in others. Through the centuries there has been a multiplication of shrines, holy places, to which people make pilgrimages in the hopes of obtaining a special blessing from God that they could not obtain anywhere else. It is common in Protestant churches to hear the church building referred to as "the house of God." It is my perception that people believe church buildings, especially the ones in which worship takes place, are especially holy. In our circles this concept is nurtured in childhood. Parents commonly warn their children to be good in church because it is God's house.

The problem is that God is thus limited to a certain holy place, and we do not have the awareness that any place can be understood as a holy place where the Christian offers thoughts and actions to God as an act of worship in accord with Paul's thought in Romans 12:1-2. Christians think God is in the church building in a way in which God is not present on the golf course. Language that would be considered inappropriate and even dangerous if used in a church building is permissible on the golf course. Actions that one would not think of taking in the sacred building are all right in the board meeting or in the classroom.

One of the problems of the English-speaking world is that we use the same noun, "church," to designate the building where the church meets as well as for the church itself, that is, the people of God. This enables one to think of one's self as separate and apart from the church rather than as an integral part of it. The church is a building on Main Street. We give to the church; we go to the church. From the view of the New Testament, however, the church is on Main Street only when that particular congregation is assembled at that location, and even then the word would refer to the people in the building and not to the building itself. At other times the church is scattered in the community. For people in general, however, the church is always on Main Street whether it is empty or filled with worshipers. If we are using the word in the New Testament sense, we do not go to the church; we assemble as the church. We do not give to the church. We participate with our brothers and sisters in sharing the financial responsibility that we as church have assumed.

On one occasion a person complained to me that his church was unfriendly. He thought of himself as separate and apart from the church with which he was associated. He had no conception of his role in the church or of his responsibility for helping the church be what he thought it ought to be. If the church was unfriendly, it was his personal problem and responsibility as a member of the group and as a contributor to whatever it was. I remarked to him that if I were pastor of the church I would ask him to take as his personal responsibility to help make the church the welcoming and friendly people they ought to be. Whatever the church's failures, each member has a responsibility for them. Because we tend to think of the church as building, however, we often fail to accept our roles and responsibilities as its members.

Personally, I refrain from using the word "sanctuary" and the phrase "house of God" to refer to the place of worship. In my opinion, house of worship or house of prayer are preferable as designations for the buildings and are more consistent with the New Testament idea of the church.

THE PRAGMATIC ISSUE

From the beginning, churches have felt the need to assemble to worship God together, to proclaim the gospel, and to address the needs of the members. If a group is going to assemble, there has to be an agreed upon place for this to happen. It can happen anywhere. Churches can come together in a home, as they commonly did in the earliest years of Christian history. They can assemble at a river for baptismal purposes, as they often did during the early days of my ministry. They can meet in a modest structure or in a costly and beautiful building. Wherever they gather, they are the church.

There is no indication in the New Testament that the earliest churches attached significance to the places where they assembled. The places were not given special names. From what we infer, most of the churches met in homes that belonged to one of the members. Such groups are often called "house churches" today (see Rom 16:5; 1 Cor 16:19; Col 4:15; Phlm 1:2). The choice of the house probably was determined more by size than anything else. The use of a house for assembly would imply that churches were small. However, a larger church in a city like Corinth could have met in several house churches.

There is no way that we can know about this or about how churches dealt with decisions forced upon them by increasing size.

When the hostility of its members forced Paul out of the synagogue in Ephesus, he moved his preaching to the lecture hall of Tyrannus (Acts 19:9). This seems to refer to Paul's public preaching but says nothing about a church forming and meeting in that building. In no instance, however, is the place of meeting called "the house of God." Indeed, judging from the New Testament texts, it would have been totally foreign to the thinking of the earliest Christians to call the meeting place by that name. The reference to place was used merely to identify the church as the group of people who assembled at a certain location.

CHURCH BUILDINGS

Another important point needs to be made. The New Testament does not speak anywhere of a church building their own house of worship. This leads to an interesting observation. Generally speaking, churches spend more money building buildings than in any other way, although this activity cannot be supported by any text from the New Testament. In times past, when I have heard pastors preach on the need to build a house of worship, which they commonly called God's house, they resorted to the Old Testament and used the texts dealing with building the temple.

The question then arises: Should churches construct buildings in which to meet? Although there is nothing in the New Testament that supports doing so, there is also no text to support the idea that we shouldn't build buildings in which to worship. It is interesting that a denomination that does not have musical instruments because there is no specific text supporting them in the New Testament has no problem with constructing and owning buildings. What the New Testament teaches is that the place where the people assemble is incidental and unimportant. The importance is attached to the nature of the group that meets there.

The issue then becomes pragmatic. Do we need to own buildings in which to meet? Is this essential to the functioning of a church in our society in this day? A number of small churches have attempted to follow the pattern of the house church of the New Testament. However, generally speaking, I do not believe that this has worked well in our society. From my observation, churches usually do better in our environment if they have appropriate structures in which to meet and function. Church life is much more complex in modern society than it was in the first century and demands different and more complex meeting places. Of course, the question of how much should be spent in this manner is another one altogether. I remember in earlier years hearing pastors, especially of small churches, condemn the Roman Catholic Church for building the cathedrals that reared themselves in splendor amid the poverty and squalor so prevalent in Latin America. Now, however, Baptist churches have their own splendid cathedrals, and we rarely hear criticism of the opulent buildings belonging to other groups.

WHAT KIND OF BUILDING?

Assuming that churches need buildings in order to function effectively in our modern society, we now face another question: What kind or kinds of buildings should the church construct? There is certainly no guidance for this issue in the texts of the New Testament. This means that we have to seek the solution through other avenues. After observing churches throughout the past several decades, I have concluded that a church generally hires an architect who will draw up a suggested design for a building. Often there seem to be two major factors involved in the final decision: (1) When people look at the building, will they know that it is a church based upon its appearance? This means that Baptist churches often follow the Jeffersonian model and are boringly alike. Apparently another criterion is the beauty of the building. (2) Will the people be appropriately impressed by the appearance of the building? The interesting point is that churches seldom, if ever, seem to ask the more important theological questions that should be considered before constructing buildings. The primary questions are these: Why does this church exist? What is its purpose? How will this building we are thinking about constructing help us achieve our purpose as a church? Several issues need to be considered. Since churches meet to worship God, one should ask how a building will facilitate the realization of that purpose. Of course, different denominations have varying approaches to worship and will, therefore, require different kinds of buildings. Because the whole approach to worship among Catholics differs drastically from Baptists and many other evangelicals, they would need a totally different kind of building.

In Baptist churches, as well as many others, the proclamation of the gospel is central to the service of worship. This means we need to ask how the church building will contribute to the effectiveness of preaching. An effective public speaker depends upon eye contact. In light of this, it is obvious that the closer the members of the congregation are to the preacher, the more effective the sermon will be. Many buildings are constructed in ways that make it impossible for the worshipers to be close to the preacher. The farther people sit from the preacher, the less effective the sermon is.

Another important factor in Baptist and many other churches is the relationship of members to one another. One may say that an underlying thesis of much that has been written here is this: God's purpose in history is to create a people who love God and love one another. The place where people worship can be constructed in a way that brings them closer together and thus contributes to achieving God's purpose for the church. On the other hand, the structure of buildings can isolate members from one another.

A good many years ago, for several months I was interim pastor of a large church with which I developed an unusual rapport. From there I went to be interim pastor of another church where I did not feel the same warmth, nor could I seem to develop the same relationship with the congregation. I thought about that a great deal, and suddenly it hit me. The difference lay, at least to a great extent, in the building. In the first building the seats were arranged in an arc so that a person sitting in one place could see the faces of the majority of the congregation. A great deal of silent communication took place among members across the distance. In the second church, the building was constructed so that members sat behind each other. Also, because of the shape of the building, the people in the first building were much closer to the pulpit. I could see their faces clearly no matter where they were seated in the building. There was much more interaction between the preacher and the congregation. The problem with many or most church buildings is that the people are seated behind each other in extended rows of pews. This seating arrangement is isolating and, therefore, antithetical both to fellowship and communication.

Another observation: For most churches the acoustics of the building are an afterthought. Only after the buildings are constructed do people turn their attention to the acoustics. Often, severe acoustical problems limit the effectiveness of whatever system is installed. I have known few churches that employed an acoustical engineer to work with the architect from the beginning to assure that the voices of those speaking or singing could be heard well.

Let me underline one of the major points of this chapter. No matter what action the church takes with regard to the construction of its buildings, a primary consideration in its decisions should be whether the completed structure will enhance or impede the church in achieving the purpose of its existence.

NOTES

[1] There are two words translated temple in the New Testament. One (*hieron*) refers to the entire temple complex; the other (*naos*) refers most of the time to the sanctuary itself to which only priests had access.

[2] Contrary to what is probably a common misperception, when the New Testament talks about Jesus going to the temple, it does not mean that Jesus was allowed to go into the sanctuary itself. Of course, as a male Jew, he was able to enter the Court of Israel where his mother, as a woman, was not allowed to go.

[3] The holiest place was the part of the sanctuary that lay behind the curtain into which the high priest alone could enter only once a year.

[4] This declaration draws on two passages found in 1 Kgs 8:27 (see also 2 Chr 2:6) and Isa 66:1, 2.

Worship: Holy Hours

Nothing in our Christian lives is more affected by tradition than the worship of our churches. The architecture of the place where we worship, the things we do in worship, and the time we worship are patterned after the practices of our mothers and fathers. Change comes slowly in these matters. Often when it does come, it leaves a considerable minority of the people disaffected and unhappy. A revision in the prayer book used for a number of generations, a new translation of the Bible, a change in the time of worship can cause immediate public relations problems. Because everything we do in worship becomes sanctified over the years, people feel that changing them somehow goes against God's will.

ASKING THE QUESTIONS

Because we often accept the way things are as God-ordained, we fail to ask the fundamental questions I think every generation needs to ask. For instance, does the church need to gather regularly as a group for public worship? Many people are vocal in their declaration that they do not need to participate in church worship services. They believe in God, they say, but they claim to be able to worship God better in private. Judging from their actions, about half the members of the average American church evidently do not believe that public worship is important. They are seldom if ever present when the church assembles for worship. Their absence is a vote against the importance of congregational worship.

Apparently the participation of believers in public worship was not a problem in the earliest days of the church's existence. In the excitement of their new experience and new relationship with brothers and sisters, they wanted to be with one another. Their response to what God did for them in Jesus was spontaneous and continuous, according to the impression the text gives. Acts tells us that the Jerusalem Christians daily "spent much time together in the temple . . . [and] broke bread at home" (2:46). They gladly joined together in their praise of God for mighty works among them.

Only one verse in the New Testament indicates that people began to neglect their attendance at congregational worship. It is found in Hebrews, a book evidently written to a group of Christians removed from the apostolic age by at least one generation (see Heb 1:1-2). In 10:25 the author urges the recipients not to neglect meeting together as some were doing. This connects us with a generation of church members more like our own, people who evidently did not respond enthusiastically to the gospel in the way so many of the first believers did. In any case, the importance of meeting together was never a real issue in New Testament times. The question as to whether the people should gather periodically to worship God could not have arisen in those times. The issue of whether they should worship together was one they did not have to discuss. Rather, they welcomed every opportunity to be together. Joy was a keynote of their gatherings.

In our time, however, the issue is forced upon us. American churches in general are troubled by their members' lack of participation in church life. People's absence from church services is the subject of many sermons and written messages. Indeed, most people are happy if the attendance one Sunday is relatively higher than it was the last Sunday. Most church buildings are not large enough to hold all the members of the church if every one of them attended on a given Sunday, which says something about our expectations. Apparently many people believe that their presence in the midst of the congregation is not an important issue. People who call themselves Christians, therefore, need to confront the issue of the importance and necessity of congregational worship in one way or the other.

Paul's theology of the church underscores the importance of our congregational gathering. He understood that something wonderful happened when the people of God came together. Something took place that did not occur in any other place and in any other circumstance. The gathered people, not the building, became the sanctuary, the holiest place, and therefore the dwelling place of the Spirit of God (1 Cor 3:16-17). The apostle's emphasis on the primacy of the prophetic gift in 1 Corinthians 12–14, for example, is linked to this concept of the assembly. When people came together, God came to dwell in their midst. The result of God's presence was the giving of the prophetic gift to one or more members of the assembly. In this way, God addressed the people to give them directions, encourage them, and admonish them. But—and this is important—it was only in the assembly that they could receive this word from God, so essential to their lives as God's people in the world.

What if people really believed they would hear from God when they gathered with their sisters and brothers for worship? It would give to them a sense of expectation and charge the whole atmosphere of the gathered church. Sadly, however, this is not the attitude of most people today. They often find public worship boring. Those present are often driven by a sense of duty rather than pulled by the expectation of something important.

I have preached in many different churches. When I appear for the first time in an unfamiliar church, I know what will occur as people drive home after the service. Someone will ask, "How did you like the preacher?" The important question is never raised: "What, if anything, did God say to you today?" What is important is not whether you liked the preacher but whether God spoke to you in some way through a word, a hymn, a prayer, a Scripture reading, or in another manner.

Does the church need to gather regularly as a group for public worship? I think most Christians would answer this question affirmatively. Even members whose actions belie their words probably would not venture to be honest and say that worship is unimportant or unnecessary in the life of the believer. That leads to a second closely related question. How often do we need to participate in congregational worship? In most Baptist churches in the deep South, the tradition of worship twice a day, Sunday mornings and evenings, is deeply ingrained. In addition, most of them have regular meetings on Wednesday evenings that include a mini worship service. For many believers reared in that tradition, churches that worship only once on Sunday are thought of as liberal or, at best, unspiritual and not dedicated. This feeling exists in spite of the fact that in earlier days of our history many of the rural churches had "preaching" only once or twice a month.

Jewish people adhered to the custom of attending the synagogue services on the Sabbath. This was the tradition inherited by the first Christians, which no doubt influenced their practice as time went on. There is nothing in the New Testament, however, that prescribes how much one should worship. We are led to believe from Acts that the earliest believers were together a great deal, perhaps every day. They did not meet without praising God, a natural and enthusiastic response to their new life in Christ. That is, their gathering was a worship service.

As the gospel moved out into the Gentile world, worship no doubt was often dictated by circumstances. One of the major factors bearing on both the frequency of worship and the time of worship was the economic situation of the members. Evidently many of them were slaves with no control over their time. Their capacity to gather with brothers and sisters in Christ was limited. Many of their meetings were likely held early in the morning before the workday began—the only time when slaves could escape from their duties.

Furthermore, there were no Christian holidays in the Roman Empire for almost 300 years. Jews occupied an unusual position according to the laws that governed them. Judaism was a legal religion, and Jews were able to observe their Sabbath. This privilege, however, did not pertain to Gentiles, and soon there were many more Gentile churches than Jewish ones. As a consequence, Christian slaves and others did not have a day off from their labors when they were free to worship. Without a doubt, the frequency of worship was not determined by the desire of believers in the first centuries of Christian history. Circumstances played an important role in the decisions churches made in this regard.

The time and frequency of worship in the churches with which I am familiar developed in a time and under circumstances far different from those of other times. When churches began meeting at least three times a week and often having revivals of one to two weeks in duration, people had a great deal more time than they have today. Few women were employed outside the homes. In the straitened social conditions of rural life, church was the center of the social life as well as the spiritual life. When churches conducted revival meetings, they usually had a 10 o'clock morning service in addition to the one in the evening. In July and August, farmers were free to attend, and the women in town or country could be present in large numbers.

To a great extent, Baptist churches in the deep South still hold to the pattern that developed in an agrarian culture, even though modern life everywhere is decidedly different. There are many more opportunities for social involvement. People are busier than ever. Most important of all, wives as well as husbands are often working. A great majority of churches in this country have adjusted their expectations somewhat to be more attuned to the circumstances in which people now live. Some churches have adopted the pattern of worship once a week. In addition, many churches of various denominations also have midweek services.

I remember thinking about this issue in 1964 as I journeyed toward a large church where I was interim pastor. I believed then, as I do now, that Sunday school was a viable organization. Also, I believed we ought to be able to expect our fellow Christians to meet with us for worship at least once a week. Furthermore, I came to the conclusion that our churches would be able to continue having midweek meetings *if* they were able to provide a meal for those who came. Mothers and fathers cannot be expected to work all day and participate in church activities if they have to go home to prepare a meal first.

Many Baptist churches in the South tend to cling to morning and evening services in spite of the drastic changes in our lives over the past forty years. For most churches, the result is that the evening services are poorly attended. Also, the people who do attend are among the most faithful of the church. They attend not because they feel a great need for an additional service on Sunday but because they are responsible members of the church.

WHEN SHOULD WE WORSHIP?

According to the book of Acts, the first Jewish Christians continued their traditional Jewish worship in addition to their meals in homes of believers (2:46; 3:1). They were reared to attend the synagogue. They were reared to observe Jewish holy days, including the Sabbath. The Gospels, nevertheless, lead us to believe that Jesus' attitude toward the Sabbath (Mark 2:23-28; 3:1-6) led him into conflict with the religious leaders of the time with reference to Sabbath observance. In order to understand their hostility to Jesus, we need to be aware that the observance of the Sabbath and circumcision were the two most distinctive characteristics of being a Jew. Any desecration of the Sabbath, therefore, was unacceptable.

The inclusion of these instances in the Gospels lead us to believe that the authors and their churches considered Jesus' attitude toward the Sabbath important. They were saying that the Jewish idea of the sacredness of the Sabbath was not acceptable to them. It was probably inevitable that believers should move toward thinking of another day as the day for Christian worship.

At some point in time, Sunday, the first day of the week, became a generally accepted day for Christian gatherings and worship. Only once in the New Testament itself is it called the Lord's day (Rev 1:10). In 1 Corinthians 16:2, Paul instructs church members to make their offering to his fund for the relief of Jewish Christians "on the first day of every week." Implicit in this instruction is the conclusion that Christians in Corinth gathered on that day for worship. That the practice of meeting on the first weekday soon became rather widespread is seen by the reference in Acts 20:7. We do not know the process by which Sunday became the time for Christians in general to gather for worship or at what point the practice became widespread. Neither does the New Testament tell us why the first day of the week became the special day for worship. The passages in Luke 24:1 and John 20:1, 19 would lead us to believe that Christians gravitated to that day because it was the day of Jesus' resurrection. Every time the church gathers, therefore, it celebrates the most important part of the gospel story.

It should be noted that the New Testament never mandates the observance of Sunday as a sacred day. I grew up, as did many of my generation, believing that there were certain things Christians did not do on Sunday, often erroneously called the Sabbath. We could not go fishing, attend movies, or participate in many other activities because we would be breaking the Sabbath. It is interesting to note that even with regard to the Sabbath the Old Testament itself has few instructions except for the general admonition found in the Commandments. Israelites were commanded to keep the Sabbath holy, which meant in part that they were not to work on that day. Subsequent to the exile when Jewish people became really committed to keeping the Sabbath, which involved avoiding work, they did not have specific rules to guide them. As a result, they began to develop a body of oral traditions designed to spell out what was permissible and what was forbidden on that day. Those commandments now constitute one large volume of the Torah. When Christians began to regard Sunday as the Christian Sabbath, they also developed traditions, one of which was the prohibition against fishing on Sunday.

Constantine changed the situation for believers in the empire in AD 321 when he issued regulations against work on Sunday. For the first time, therefore, Christians were free to choose the time of day or night when they would gather for worship on Sunday. Nevertheless, Sunday was never called the Sabbath before the eleventh century. It remained for John Knox and other Scotch and English reformers to create Sabbatarianism in the strictest form, the kind that became a part of the tradition of American Christianity. The earliest settlers in Massachusetts brought it to the New World where they enacted strict "blue laws." This was a major influence in Baptist churches in the South, such as the kind in which I was reared.

EVERY DAY IS HOLY

A text that bears directly on this discussion is found in Colossians 2:16: "Therefore do not let anyone condemn you in matters of food and drink or observing festivals, new moons, or sabbaths." Some teachers in Colossae were evidently attempting to get the church as a whole to adopt certain Jewish practices in the expression of their faith, and among these was the observation of the Jewish holy days.[1] Paul took the position that such a practice was foreign to genuine Christianity. No day was holier than any other.

This leads us to one of the major failures of legalism. Many people think that the problem with legalism is that it is too demanding. To the contrary, one weakness of legalism is that it does not demand enough in terms of faith and practice (see Matt 5:20). When we make one day holier than others, we compartmentalize our lives. We give the holy day or a part of it to God, but we can keep the other six days for ourselves. From the Christian perspective, every day is holy. In Romans 12:1-2 Paul called upon the Roman Christians to offer their bodies as living sacrifices to God. Body in this context means all that we do and all that we think. The individual Christian is a temple of the Spirit of God where worship takes place daily. All of life—our relationships, our work, our play—is an offering to God.

In religions that emphasize holy days, the deity is offended if we desecrate the sacredness of the day by going against the rules. In Christianity, we dishonor God if what we do is unworthy of our Redeemer and Lord *whenever we do it*. Anything that does not dishonor or, better, honors God is permissible on any day of the week. Anything that we can do as Christians on any one day is certainly permissible on any other day.

CONCLUSION

In conclusion, worship is just as valid on Tuesday as it is on Sunday or the Sabbath. When the congregation determines a time for the people to gather in congregational worship, the important factor is defining particular circumstances. Most Christian churches have set their worship services on Sunday. That is certainly an appropriate and significant day to meet to praise God for the gift of life through the resurrected Christ. Generally speaking, it is the day when more members are free to engage in worship. As I was growing up, our church met at the traditional morning and evening hours, even though about half the men worked shift work and were unable to attend on any given Sunday. As far as I know, no real thought was ever given to alternate days of worship to meet their need. It was difficult for the church to think outside the box.

During the fuel crisis a few years ago, driving was curtailed by law in Belgium on Sundays to conserve fuel. That made it impossible for many of the members of the Baptist church to assemble on the Lord's day. The church decided to meet for worship on an evening when there were no driving restrictions, which was an appropriate response to the circumstances of that time. The worship on that night was just as valid as it was when the church met on Sundays.

What is wrong with playing golf on Sundays? Nothing, if there is nothing wrong with that activity and the way you do it on Monday. But there is another aspect of the question that we must consider. What is wrong with playing golf when your fellow believers have gathered to worship and praise God? The problem is not that you have desecrated the Sabbath. The problem is that you have acted in an irresponsible and pagan manner. When an individual is a member of a congregation that has decided the time of worship will be on Sunday morning, each member of the congregation is as responsible as every other member to participate in that worship. By playing golf instead, you indicate that the activity is more important to you than worshiping God. If every other member were as irresponsible as you are, the knowledge of the gospel would soon perish from the earth. As someone has said, Christianity is always only a generation away from extinction.

NOTE

[1] The evidence leads to the conclusion that the so-called Colossian heresy was a syncretism of influences from various sources, including Judaism and Gnosticism.

Christianity and the State

It is a gross mistake to assume that the relationship between Christianity and government in America can be compared in any way to what existed in the early history of the Christian movement. The relationship between church and state as defined in the first amendment to the constitution was something altogether new in human history. According to the constitution of the United States, congress can make no law respecting the establishment of religion or prohibiting its free exercise. That was a first when it was implemented, and it is still a foreign concept in many countries of the world. The idea of a free church in a free state, therefore, is of recent origin in the world's history. Prior to the adoption of our constitution, no government had ever accepted the principle that its sole duty with regard to religion was to prohibit interference in the free operation of the religious institutions within its boundary. Even a colony like Massachusetts, whose original settlers came to these shores to escape religious persecution, was extremely intolerant regarding the rights of others.

OLD TESTAMENT

The ideal in the Old Testament is exactly the opposite of the modern American ideal. In Old Testament times, there was a complete identity between the nation and the people of God. There was no distinction between religious and criminal or civil law. All law, dealing with whatever issue, was an expression of God's will for the people of God. The breaking of any law was an offense against God and the punishment was an expression of the divine will. God was considered the genuine ruler of Israel, and the king was the instrument through which God ruled the people. Of course, the history of the people indicates that the reality, generally speaking, fell far short of the ideal.

At the dawn of the Christian era, Jews were ruled by the Romans, and their ideal of the nation had become a dream for the future, something that would be brought about by God. In the meantime, they enjoyed unusual freedom granted to them by the Roman government. Julius Caesar was friendly toward the Jews, and under his rule the terms of Jewish existence were clearly defined. Judaism was a legal religion (*religio licito*), granted the privilege of observing the Sabbath, having exemption from military service, establishing synagogues, transferring monies to Jerusalem, and enjoying other rights.

With reference to the Jewish people the Roman government was primarily concerned about the collection of taxes and the maintenance of control over the territories under her hegemony. Otherwise, the supervision of the Jewish communities was largely a matter for their courts, which were headed, of course, by the great Sanhedrin in Jerusalem. The government, therefore, granted whatever privileges the Jews enjoyed. This system was totally unrelated to any idea of religious liberty as a right and the belief that people in general should be able to pursue their own religious ideas under the protection of the state.

In the earliest days, Roman rulers did not distinguish between Jews and Christians. At least to some extent, Christianity thus enjoyed operating under the cloak of religious liberty granted to the Jews. For example, Gallio, proconsul of Achaia, rejected a charge brought by Jews against Paul in Jerusalem on the grounds that the matter was not an issue appropriate for Roman courts (Acts 18:12ff.). Rather, it was a matter for Jews to take care of themselves.

NEW TESTAMENT

When we search the New Testament for texts that detail the relationship of Christians and the state in those earliest years, we find very few, and they reflect three different views regarding this matter. We shall examine each of those texts in turn.

Jesus

In general, taxes are never popular with people anywhere. They are even more unpopular when, as was the case with first-century Jews in Palestine, they are levied by a ruling foreign power. The Roman government exacted several kinds of taxes. Taxes, which could be classified as customs, were imposed on goods conveyed on highways or on goods entering or leaving the cities. Responsibility for collecting such taxes was contracted by the Roman government. The contractors or publicani often employed local nationals to impose the tax. This system was open to flagrant abuse, and the opportunity for enriching oneself in the process of collecting the duties was universally exploited. The hated tax collectors mentioned in the New Testament, such as Matthew and Zacchaeus, were classified with prostitutes as the worst among sinners. People held no hope for their redemption because it was thought impossible for them to make restitution for all the wrongs they had committed through their years of collecting taxes.

The most despised of all the taxes, however, was the poll tax levied on the Jewish people under the rule of the emperor Augustus. A census was necessarily conducted to serve as the basis for collecting the tax. This census provoked a violent, ill-fated uprising, led by a certain Judas of Galilee referred to in Acts 5:37. It is thought that the Jewish extremists referred to as zealots had their beginning in this uprising. More than any others, the poll tax brought home to Jews the ignominy of their subservient role as a conquered people. It was a constant reminder of the extent to which they had fallen since the glorious days of independence.

This poll tax was the one at issue in the confrontation with Jesus described in Mark 12:13-17 and in the parallel passages (Matt 22:15 and Luke 20:20-26). The question with which Jesus' enemies challenged him was whether or not the Jewish law, that is, the word of God, allowed Jews to pay the tax or prohibited it. From the point of view of the Jewish extremists (the zealots) and many others, payment of the tax was an egregious expression of disloyalty to God. On the other side stood the power of the Roman government that was intolerant of resistance to the payment of taxes. Jesus' enemies thought of the question as a clever way to place him squarely between these two opposing forces. They felt that any answer would invoke either the hostility of the people or the wrath of the Roman authorities.

In order to understand Jesus' reply to his adversaries, we need to know something about the monetary system of the times. One of the responsibilities of a ruling power was the provision of a monetary means of exchange. The use of those coins by people in a region expressed their recognition of the ruler's sovereignty. Furthermore, the coins were deemed the property of the ruler under whose authority they were minted and distributed. These circumstances lie behind the request Jesus made of his interrogators for a coin, which, as was acknowledged by his enemies, bore the image of Tiberius, the reigning sovereign, and the superscription "Tiberius, Caesar, son of the divine Augustus." In Syria the coin also added "the majestic son of God."

The possession of the coin by Jesus' adversaries and their use of it as a medium of exchange were a public admission that they recognized the emperor, who was Tiberius at the time, as sovereign over that territory. According to the accepted patterns of the time, the coin had been minted under Caesar's authority and circulated by him. Thus, they answered their own question, which Jesus made clear. Elementary morality called for an individual to return property that belonged to another when requested to do so. The poll tax could be understood as an official request for the people to return Caesar's coin, which they had in their purses.

The second part of Jesus' statement, however, was probably unexpected. Jesus cautioned: "[Give] to God the things that are God's." The adversaries had planned what they thought was a clever trap. Not only was the trap rendered harmless, but they were also confronted with a decisive word from God for their own lives. It could well be that the admonition Jesus gave was triggered by a claim on the coin that Tiberius was divine. Having that coin in their possession was actually a violation of the second commandment as interpreted by the Jews. It violated the command against having graven images. The emperor could make certain legitimate demands on the people under his sovereignty. Only God, however, had a claim on their ultimate allegiance.

One of the problems with this very brief, laconic passage is that it does not spell out for Christians the exact boundary between Caesar's claims and God's claims. For this reason, Christian thinking about the issue has been diverse. Indeed, thinking individuals all probably have a different point at which they would be willing to deny the claims of the state and risk its wrath and the opprobrium of fellow citizens on the basis of their loyalty to God. In the context of the biblical passage, the only clear truth is that Jesus did not side with the zealots and other extreme nationalists in their understanding that payment of the poll tax was a denial of the claims of God. Furthermore, Jesus warned that there was a limit to the loyalty Caesar should receive.

Paul

In Romans 13:1-7, Paul spells out his attitude about the relationship between Christians and the Roman government. Let us first establish two points. First, Paul's attitude toward the Roman government was positive. This no doubt arose out of his own experience. That experience was not uniformly good, as is evident in his comments in 2 Corinthians 11:23.[1] Roman authorities had mistreated him at various times. However, Paul did not have the expectations of his government that we have of ours, and the negative experiences did not outweigh the positive ones. He was able to travel over a vast territory, united under the rule of Rome and generally at peace. Usually he could count on the protection of that government. For the purpose of his mission, the most important factor in shaping his attitude, there had never been a more propitious time for the spread of the gospel by an itinerant missionary.

In the second place, Paul knew that the government of Rome was a pagan government. Indeed, it was impossible for him to imagine that anyone claiming to be Christian would ever rule over the empire. The group with which he identified himself was a microscopic minority in that vast Mediterranean world. At the same time, the small number of Christians in his world did not determine his perspective because his trust was in God and in God's power rather than human forces.

Although his world was a pagan world for the most part, Paul did not believe God was totally inactive in that sphere. God had instruments who, consciously or not, were being used to serve the Creator in a hostile world. If not, total chaos would have been the consequence of unleashed evil unchecked by God. There was, however, a certain amount of order in the sinful world. Paul attributed that order to God's acting through the government officials who were humanly responsible for maintaining the order.

A reading of the Romans passage shows that Paul defined the role of the state as the servant of God rather carefully. This aspect of Paul's discussion has been overlooked with disastrous consequences. Those familiar with the history of the west know that kings and emperors based their claim to unchallenged authority, often abused with consequent suffering by helpless subjects, on a wrong understanding of the Romans passage. This doctrine, called "the divine right of kings," was based on their interpretation of Romans and a few other passages. Rulers claimed that the indiscriminate exercise of total power by rulers was a prerogative granted to them by God. It was, therefore, a grievous sin for subjects to oppose the king. This thinking governed political philosophy in Europe for many centuries. The position of the founding fathers was exactly the opposite. Our nation was founded on the notion that people, not their rulers, were sovereign and that leaders held office at the pleasure of the people.

To understand his true thinking on the issue, we need to notice how Paul limited the role of the emperor as the servant of God in Romans 13:3-5. Governing authorities act as servants of God to protect the person who does good. They also act as servants of God when they punish those who do wrong. Paul could never have defined the authorities as God's servants when they did evil things, as they often did. In verse 5 we find the same implication. If Christians followed the leading of conscience, according to Paul, they would not incur the wrath of the ruler because they would be doing what was right. This statement is based on the assumption that the ruler is fulfilling his God-given role of maintaining order in a just society.

The Romans passage leaves the modern believer in the same situation that Jesus' teaching does. Christians have to decide for themselves if their governing authorities are demanding conduct of them that is contrary to their understanding of God's will for their lives. Thus, for example, many believers refused to obey the demands of the government when they were drafted during the Vietnamese war. Many church members refused to respect the decisions of the government with regard to the prosecution of that war. Of course, this placed many of them in the position of suffering the consequences of their actions when the authorities acted to punish them. In addition, they suffered the opprobrium of their fellow citizens. On the other hand, many Christians in America supported the war because they saw it as an essential step in stopping the tide of atheistic communism that was such a threat to the world after World War II. This illustrates that there is no escaping the subjective dimensions with regard to our decisions about obeying the governing authorities.

According to Paul, Christians had three obligations to the governing authorities of their day. The first is one with which Christians should not have a problem. They were to lead the kind of life that would not bring the wrath of the authorities upon them. That is, they were to be what we know as "law-abiding citizens." They had the obligation not to commit what we would call criminal acts. When the authorities functioned as servants of God, they did not require actions that would go against simple morality. Also, when they functioned as servants of God, they protected the people who were innocent of wrongdoing from the wrongdoers. In the second place, believers were to pay the taxes demanded by the state. Citizens who enjoy the benefit of living in a society that is both orderly and relatively good have a responsibility to help bear the financial burden involved in the state's actions. In the third place, Christians were to respect the ruling authorities. That, however, is not an unusual thing to expect of Christians. When believers act as believers, they respect all other people. Respect for the emperor in that day or for the president, senator, or judge of our day is a natural expression of the Christian's attitude toward all people. Of course, this does not mean that we must agree with the decisions of our elected officials or that we support them politically. On the other hand, citizens acting as Christians never treat leaders with the kind of disrespect so commonly witnessed in our society.

First Peter

In 1 Peter 2:13 the author gives his advice to Christians about their relationship to the Roman government. As you can see immediately, that advice simply parallels what we have read in Paul's epistle to the Romans. According to some interpretations of 1 Peter, the Christians addressed in the letter are being subjected to governmental persecution. That understanding, however, is open to question. Nevertheless, whatever our conclusion, the attitude toward the emperor and his officials expressed in the epistle is positive.

Officials are the servants of God, but once again the author limits that by his description of the role of the officials as servants. They "punish those who do wrong" and "praise those who do right" (1 Pet 2:14). The opposite situation is not addressed in the letter. However, 1 Peter 3:13-17 offers guidance about how Peter may have dealt with that. If Christians are to suffer, they should suffer for doing right, that is, for being faithful to their commitment to the Lord no matter what the consequence.

Revelation

The last book in the New Testament expresses a totally different attitude toward the Roman government than what we find in the passages mentioned above. The reason lies in the radically different circumstances experienced by the author of Revelation in his relationship to the government.

According to official Roman policy, an emperor did not become a god until after his death when the Roman senate could make the decision to elevate him to that ethereal level. However, especially in the eastern part of the empire, people had long believed that heroes and people who occupied elevated positions were at least descendants of the gods. This was a way of understanding the reason for the difference between those who reigned at the top of society and the ordinary people under them. A number of the emperors actively encouraged the belief that they were divine along with the development of the emperor cultus with its temples and priests. One of these was Domitian (AD 81–96), who many scholars believe was the emperor at the time of the writing of Revelation. The book was evidently written to encourage the Christians of Asia Minor in a time when they felt tremendous pressure to join the rest of the inhabitants by participating in the cult of emperor worship. We can understand something of the pressure these believers felt when we recognize that failure to participate marked them as strange and recalcitrant and branded them as disloyal to the emperor.

The worship of the emperor and Rome was the one universal cult in Asia Minor where many different deities claimed the devotion of inhabitants. Promoters of the cult were not concerned about how many gods an individual had. It did matter a great deal if one of those gods was not the emperor. For Christians, however, faithfulness to Christ meant that they had no other Lord besides him, no other God except the one they had come to know through the revelation of Christ. To participate in worship of the emperor did not interfere with the pagans' worship of their other gods. For Christians, the opposite was true. Participation in emperor worship meant nothing less than renunciation of Christ as their Lord. For them the choice was not Christ and Caesar. It was Christ or Caesar.

John's View of the Roman Government

The attitude of John[2] toward the Roman government is clearly depicted in the vivid images of Revelation 12 and 13. The dragon, cast out of heaven by Michael and the angels, is identified as "the Devil and Satan, the deceiver of the whole world" (12:9). The "beast rising out of the sea" (13:1) is the Roman Empire, its heads representing the several Roman emperors. Note the contrast between the author's views and Paul's as seen clearly in 13:4. The emperor was not the servant of God in the exercise of governing power. Rather, he had been granted his authority by the dragon or Satan. In other words, imperial power was arrayed against God in the church and was the devil's instrument to carry out his purpose of destroying the church. The governing authorities' actions could not possibly be understood as fulfilling their roles as God's servants for good.

In 13:11ff. another beast is depicted, this one rising out of the earth. The role of this beast is to force people to worship the emperor. Apparently this is a depiction of the priests of the imperial cult, the ones responsible in various locales along with governors and other officials for putting Christians under pressure to abandon their allegiance to the Lord. The book of Revelation was written to encourage and inspire Christians of that day to be true to their Lord no matter the consequence. They were assured that God and not Satan was sovereign. They could be confident that the final victory belonged to God and not to the empire and that they would be vindicated. They had nothing to fear, not even death itself.

Conclusion

The passages from Revelation do not give us clear guidelines for the relationship between Christians and the state. We still are faced with the necessity of making our own judgments when confronted with a conflict between the claims of the state and what we believe to be the claims of God to our allegiance.

The problem is that few of us go along entirely with all the decisions made by our government. A part of the taxes we pay will always go to causes or institutions that we do not believe are good. The government will pass laws we think are wrong or fail to pass laws we think a humane state should adopt. The truth of the matter is that no government has ever existed or ever will exist in which all the ideals of any Christian are realized. Societies are relatively just or unjust. Some are more just than others, and Christians, as Christians, have the obligation of working to promote a greater degree of justice and compassion.

Our situation differs totally from that of Jesus and his earliest followers. They had no say in whether a tax was levied or not. They had no right to protest. The only action they could take was that of rebellion against the state, the position advocated by the Zealots. Of course, most people at the time realized that such a course was suicidal. Even when the Jewish people were finally drawn into rebellion against the Empire with the disastrous results of which we are aware, the majority of the people wanted to accommodate the Romans. A vociferous and fanatic minority can cause people to be plunged into conflicts they do not want. There are enough modern examples to illustrate that.

The question Jesus confronted was whether the payment of the tax involved disloyalty to God or whether it mattered in one's relationship to God. From Jesus' point of view, the payment of the tax said nothing about one's relationship to God. However, he warned his interrogators that people are always in danger of not giving to God that which belongs to God, primarily themselves.

From Paul's point of view, order was important. He lived in a day when there was more order in the Mediterranean world than had ever existed there. People were freer to live their lives, engage in commerce, and move from place to place than they had ever been before. Also, Paul was relatively free to carry out his commitment to preach the gospel in every part of the Empire. Once again, the tiny minority of Christians in the Roman Empire had absolutely no opportunity to affect the laws under which they lived. The challenge they faced was to live as Christians in a totalitarian state. Many Christians today have to live out their lives in similar circumstances. In Romans 13 Paul mentioned three obligations they had: (1) obey laws against criminal behavior; (2) pay their taxes; (3) respect the governing authorities.

However, to John the state was the enemy of God, the special tool of Satan in the war against God and the followers of Jesus. Rebellion was not advocated. Christians were helpless under the power of Rome. He advocated the only course he saw open to Christians in the circumstances. No matter how powerful the forces of government arrayed against them, they were to be faithful to their Lord, even if it cost them their own lives. His hope for the future did not rest in the tiny groups of Christians scattered over Asia Minor but in the power of God. As powerful as Satan was at the moment, John proclaimed that God was still sovereign and that the final victory belonged to their God and to the Christian disciples. The central message to believers living under a great deal of pressure is found in this exhortation: "Be faithful until death, and I will give you the crown of life" (Rev 2:10b).

Our Options

Small groups in this country are convinced that our government is totally evil. From time to time we see the tragic evidence of that, such as the bombing of the government building in Oklahoma City. On the other hand, the great majority of Americans would be more comfortable adopting a view similar to Paul's in Romans 13. Although our governmental system is admittedly flawed and will always be flawed, we believe that it deserves our support.

A minority of Christians living under the Nazi regime came to have the same judgment about their government that the writer of Revelation had about the Roman Empire. They concluded that the state had become demonic, an evil entity to which they could not give their loyalty. They even reached the conclusion that it would be better to kill Hitler than to allow him to live. Outstanding Christian leaders, such as Dietrich Bonhoeffer and Martin Niemoeller, were part of the plot to do that. The difficult decisions in life come not in the choice between good and evil but in situations in which we are confronted by only two options, that which is bad and that which is worse. This kind of choice lay before those courageous members of the Confessing Church.

We come back to emphasize that the situation of citizens in this country vis-à-vis their government is unlike anything we find in the New Testament. It could not have been conceived of prior to the American Revolution. With the birth of the American nation, for the first time in history people had the privilege of electing the individuals who would govern them. Those who presided over the affairs of this nation were not to rule by divine right but by the will of the people. Except in limited cases, we do not have the direct responsibility of actually crafting and passing laws. However, those who do pass and sign laws are subject to our wishes and can be removed at the next election if we disapprove of them. That is the power of the ballot. This means that we as individuals are each responsible to some extent if our country is unjust and inhumane. We bear individual guilt for the collective evil of our American society.

There are other aspects of a modern democracy that were not foreseen in the earliest church. No one in the New Testament could conceive of a Christian being the ruler of the empire. Although in those early days a few officials evidently were converted, they were insignificant in the total scheme of things. In this country, on the other hand, Christians are elected to the presidency and congress; they are chosen to be policemen; they are generals and admirals. How can a person be a Christian and at the same time serve as sheriff? How can a person be faithful to Christ and at the same time serve as president of a country that contains atheists, agnostics, Jews, Muslims, and members of almost every other religious group of any size? After all, he is their president also. These and many other questions clamor for answers that are not easy to come by.

A concluding word: No country ever has been or ever will be totally just and humane. That is true of this country. In spite of its faults, most of us are exceedingly thankful that we are citizens of this country rather than Haiti, Afghanistan, or some other area of our world where human suffering is so pronounced. Furthermore, one responsibility we have as Christians is clear. We have the opportunity and solemn responsibility to work unceasingly to help move our country nearer to the ideal of a totally just society.

NOTES

[1] ". . . I am talking like a madman—I am a better one: with far greater labors, far more imprisonments, with countless floggings, and often near death." Beating by a rod was a punishment decreed by a Roman official.

[2] We know the writer was named John (Rev 1:1). Scholars disagree, however, whether the traditional identification of this John with the apostle John is correct.

The Mission of the Church

In Acts 1:8 we read: "you will be my witnesses in Jerusalem, in all Judea and Samaria, and to the ends of the earth." According to Acts, this is a summary statement of the will of Jesus for his followers. It is a good place to begin a discussion of the church's mission in the world and to the world.

THE NATURE OF THE GOSPEL AND THE MISSION OF THE CHURCH

Notice that the nature of the church's mission arises out of the character of the gospel, the good news of God's redemption in Jesus Christ. At the center of this good news is an event—the good tidings of God's offered redemption in Jesus Christ. In its larger dimensions, the gospel is the story of the life, deeds, message, death, and resurrection of Jesus.[1] The larger event is reduced to an absolute minimum in Paul's summary statement in 1 Corinthians 15:3: "For I handed on to you as of first importance what I in turn had received: that Christ died for our sins in accordance with the scriptures, and that he was buried, and that he was raised on the third day in accordance with the scriptures."

The meaning of the larger event, the Incarnation, came into sharp focus for Paul in that one event at the end of Jesus' life, his crucifixion on a Roman cross, condemned as a rebel against the rule of Tiberius Caesar. Crucifixion was a rather commonplace event in the Hellenistic world ruled by the Romans, especially in Palestine, a turbulent corner of the empire. Some Jews, especially Galileans, were always stirring up unrest in their hostility to Roman overlords. One more Galilean insurrectionist dying by the decree of Pontius Pilate, the Roman governor of Judea, did not change the daily lives of most people. In the larger Gentile world, nobody took notice of the affair.

A more unlikely occurrence could not have been chosen to become the most decisive, significant happening in human history. Yet this is the incredible claim made by those first disciples. The radical view of the death of Jesus came into being because the first disciples were convinced that Jesus appeared to them after his death. They believed everything that happened before and since the death and resurrection of Jesus took its meaning from that event. Here human beings came into contact with the most decisive revelation of God in human history. Only in the light of that event could one begin to understand what God was about in the world.[2]

As we saw in our discussion of apostleship, the earliest followers of Jesus had a special privilege and responsibility because of their relationship to Jesus. They were first-person witnesses—witnesses of his words, his deeds, his death, and his resurrection. Because of their experience with Jesus they had become privy to God's great mystery, the divine plan to overcome the alienation of sin and bring hostile humans into a reconciled relationship with their Creator.[3] Just a handful of people knew what the world did not know and what God wanted it to know. Their responsibility was to start a human chain of witnesses by telling their story to as many people as possible.

UNLIKELY WITNESSES

The scope of their mission is made clear in Acts 1:8. They were to tell the story in Jerusalem, all Judea, Samaria, and to the ends of the earth. From any perspective, the magnitude of that task was incredible. Apparently those first witnesses were not overawed by the size of it. With our modern polls, we are probably much more conscious of the impossibility of our mission than they were. However, neither they nor we were given the responsibility for the successful execution of the total task. We are to be faithful witnesses where we are in the circumstances and opportunities given to us, however limited they may be. We are to trust God to use us in the eternal plan of redemption.

From the book of Acts and certain remarks in Paul's letters, one gets the idea that those first disciples had a great deal to overcome in order to reach the world. The first witnesses were a group of prejudiced Jews who, according to Acts, had to be forced on occasion to break through the wall of their prejudice for the sake of the mission. Going to Samaria from any place in Judea was easy even in the ancient world, when many people traveled on foot. Samaria was close to the earliest disciples physically, but in another sense Samaria was on the other side of the world. Jews despised Samaritans, and that attitude had been ingrained in those earliest disciples since birth. If I were given the task of choosing people to be the earliest witnesses to the gospel, a group of Jews with their inbred negative attitude toward Gentiles would have been my last resort. Rather, I would have chosen Stoics whose concept of our common humanity was much nearer to the Christian ideal.[4] How like God to choose the most unlikely people to be the bearers of the gospel story!

THE REVELATION AS EVENT

The belief that an event in history is the crucial aspect of God's revelation to humankind is both the glory and scandal of the gospel. It is the glory of the gospel because it makes God accessible to anybody who hears about it. At the center of the good news of God's redeeming grace is a story. You do not have to possess an impressive I.Q., a theological education, or any education at all for that matter in order to understand a story. The story can be told in the villages of interior Africa, in the remote reaches of the Amazon Valley, in the Eskimo settlements of the Arctic, or to children anywhere; and these hearers can understand it. Children can be Christians. I have told people through the years that I believed more fully at the age of nine than I ever have since then. Mentally retarded people can be Christians. Simple-minded folk can be Christians. The gospel cuts across human boundaries of culture and education because it is essentially a story.

At the same time, the character of the "gospel as event" is in a sense its greatest problem. If the Christian faith offered were a concept about God or man, we could assume that other people living in other places would have the insight to perceive the truth of that concept. I have talked to people from other religious groups who assured me that their concept about God was similar to the Christian idea. When I maintained that God was love, they could not have agreed with me more fervently.

Nevertheless, the Christian gospel does not simply assert a concept about God. Rather, it declares, "In this is love, not that we loved God but that he loved us and sent his Son to be the atoning sacrifice for our sins" (1 John 4:10). The Christian gospel says that all our notions about love—be it human or divine—are inadequate at best or corrupt at worst. It says that we have to know the story in order to understand the depth of God's love for us. It also declares that God's love becomes a power that transforms our lives when we trust the man who died on the cross.

Therefore, a concept does not stand at the center of the gospel. An event does. This means that people can share in the benefits and power of that event only if someone tells them about it. Events cannot have meaning and impact in the lives of other people unless they are reported. We saw a powerful illustration of this truth in the terrible events that took place in New York and Washington on September 11, 2001. Those of us who saw those planes commandeered by terrorists ram into the World Trade Towers and the Pentagon were greatly affected by the event. Such things would happen quite apart from the communications media that report on them daily, but they would not be a part of my life if someone were not telling the story. I would be blissfully ignorant of the deaths of so many people, the sorrow of survivors, and all the consequences that still flow from the event. Because someone told me the story, however, I also share in the experience. Sadness, horror, and a sense of responsibility for the situation are part of my experience because I have heard.

A CHAIN OF WITNESSES

So it is with the gospel. People can share in the meaning of the Christ event only if it is reported. The church of which I am a part today, along with all other Christian churches, traces its origin to those days after the crucifixion of Jesus when the people who had followed him and witnessed his ministry and death came to believe that he had appeared to them alive. With that belief, everything changed. Despair gave way to hope; defeat gave way to a vision of unlimited possibilities; depression gave way to boundless optimism; cowardice gave way to unbelievable courage. They had a story to tell to a world that had not heard it. They began to tell the story to everyone who would listen. People heard it and believed it. Their lives were also changed. As a result, they too had a story to tell. Their witness was added to that of the earliest disciples. Some early Christians wrote the story, and miraculously those documents were preserved. And so it went down through the years, down through the centuries in an ever-widening chain of storytellers until it came to me and became my story.

My personal testimony, which I often gave in the opening class of first-year students, is this: I believe in God, and I believe in the God I have come to know in Jesus of Nazareth. This is my story. I am not a Hindu; I am not a Buddhist; I am not a Muslim. They also have a story, but it is not my story. I am a Christian because my faith in God began with hearing the story about Jesus preserved in the New Testament and witnessed to by the people among whom I grew to adulthood.

I believe in God. However, a question arises. In what kind of God do I believe? To say I believe in a God whom I came to know through the story of Jesus means I believe in a God of incredible grace whose love goes out to all human beings. The God I know through Jesus accepts a Zacchaeus, a tax collector despised by his fellows and excluded from their social circles, a man considered beyond redemption because he defrauded so many people. However, Jesus showed that God accepted a Zacchaeus, making no demands, asking for nothing in return. The God I know accepts the wayward prodigal who in desperation returns home—accepts him without recriminations, without blame, without demands. The God Jesus reveals to me accepts women, all kinds of women, and makes them feel valued. When I say I believe in the God I have learned about through Jesus, that is the kind of God I am talking about. That God is a God of incredible grace and boundless love. If I err in the way I tell my story, I want to err on the side of grace.

PEOPLE WHO HAVE NOT HEARD

The center of the gospel is a historic event. The only way we can know it, as emphasized above, is for someone who knows about it to tell us. This gives rise to a question that troubles Christians. Countless times people have asked me that question: What is God going to do about the multiplied millions of people who have lived and died without ever hearing the Christian story? Does this mean that they have no opportunity for redemption? Many people seem to feel that they can speak for God, but I am not one of them. Any opinion I offer about what God is going to do about anybody is totally out of place. Only God knows the answers to these kinds of questions. My personal theology forces me to leave all the decisions about judgment and salvation in God's hands. I am convinced, however, that the God in whom I believe can be trusted to act in the way portrayed in the life of Jesus. That God calls the religious establishment into judgment, is identified with the outsider, and has a special love for the neglected people of the world.

I do not need to make final judgments about other people, whatever the situation. I need to be true to the trust I have received, true to the person I am, true to the story that has shaped my life. My sole responsibility is to tell the story. Admittedly, telling the story takes many forms. Of course, it is told verbally. However, it can be told without saying a word through our humility, our love manifested in concrete acts, our commitment to family, and in many other ways. It is then the responsibility of the people who hear the story to respond to it in the way that they deem best. It is not mine to pass judgment on the people to whom I tell my story.

My wife and I spent almost ten years of our lives in Brazil as missionaries. Brazil is the largest country in world in which the majority of the population ostensibly belongs to the Roman Catholic Church. This often means little more than that they were baptized into that church as infants. However, many of them had no personal religious commitment and were open to other possibilities. For example, Spiritism is a major religion in Brazil. This is an eclectic religion that draws from different religious sources including animism, which lies in the background of the population that came from Africa.

Other evangelical churches have found Brazil a fruitful soil for their proclamation of the gospel. Pentecostalism seems to have a special appeal and has grown by leaps and bounds, as it has in other Latin American countries. During my years in Brazil, I preached all over the country. I confess that my attitude toward other Christian denominations was not as broad as it became as the years went by. I know now that genuine faith cuts across all historical boundaries and that some of the greatest Christians in the world are Roman Catholic. Some of those great Christians lived in Brazil. In the same way, I know that every denomination has what we call "nominal" members among its constituents. Baptists also count among their members huge numbers of people who do not appear to have a meaningful faith and have no story to tell.

Whatever my attitude toward Roman Catholics in Brazil at the time, I do not believe that I ever condemned their church in my preaching. Even in my more immature days, I recognized that I was not preaching to judge the members of my audience. Mine was a positive message. I was there to tell my story. I had the privilege of telling my hearers about the man who lived two thousand years ago, my perception of the kind of person he was, how he died on a cross, my conviction that he triumphed over death and was alive, and my belief that I had a relationship with the God he revealed because of what he had been and done. If someone in the audience did not have a satisfying personal faith in God, I hoped that hearing my story would make a difference. I could not look into their hearts to know what they were thinking, the kind of people they were, or what their specific needs were. Whatever I might say about them would not make any difference. They had to respond to the gospel in terms of their own needs, hopes, and fears. After I told my story, it was up to them to decide whether they needed to react to it and what they needed to do. They had to decide in the light of my testimony if what I said had any relevance to their lives and their relationship with God. Over and over, throughout the years of my ministry, people have heard my story and some have embraced faith in the God revealed in Jesus of Nazareth and have become my brothers and sisters in God's family. As a result, they have their own story to tell.

OTHER RELIGIONS

One fundamental Christian belief is that there is only one God. We are not the only religion in the world to accept that belief. Jews and Muslims, of course, have as a basic tenet of their faith that there is only one God. Indeed, their monotheism is not complicated by the trinitarian concept of God central to orthodox Christianity. This question arises in connection with our discussion: Is it possible for people to know and have a relationship with this one God through religions rather than through the revelation presented by Jesus?

Once again, when this question arises, I take refuge in the position that I do not know and cannot know the answer. Furthermore, it is not my responsibility to deal with that issue. It is God's responsibility and God's alone. I take seriously certain New Testament texts about our inability to judge, beginning with the one in the Sermon on the Mount found in Matthew 7:1: "Do not judge, so that you may not be judged." There is also a relevant text written by Paul at 1 Corinthians 4:5: "Therefore, do not pronounce judgment before the time, before the Lord comes, who will bring to light the things now hidden in darkness and will disclose the purposes of the heart." There are several reasons why we should hesitate in making judgments about others. We don't know enough, and we are not good enough to judge. Furthermore, when we make judgments, we remove ourselves from our appropriate position before God as those who, along with all of humanity, are responsible to God for our lives.

When the question about the possibility of knowing God apart from Jesus is raised, people normally quote Scripture. We can quote several verses to defend the exclusiveness of the Christian revelation. A notable one is Acts 4:12: "There is salvation in no one else, for there is no other name under heaven given among mortals by which we must be saved." My only response when people quote such texts is that that even with the Bible I am not God. God and God alone draws the lines and makes final judgments.

Paul makes an interesting statement in 2 Corinthians 5:11: "Therefore, knowing the fear of the Lord, we try to persuade others . . . ." In other words, his evangelistic efforts were motivated by his understanding that he was responsible to God for what he knew and what he had received. Often preachers depict the fate of a lost world in more or less lurid terms in their attempt to motivate people to give themselves and what they have to the spreading of the gospel in the world. However, it appears to me that such appeals are largely ineffective, given the limited response of most church members. There are certainly exceptions, but few church members give sacrificially or get seriously involved in missions personally. One would think that people who believe the fate of people without the gospel is as dire as generally predicted would be willing to give whatever they have and go anywhere in the attempt to get the gospel to them.

What should motivate me, however, is not what God may or may not do to someone else. Rather, it is my own personal responsibility before God to be true to what I claim to be at the center of my life. I am responsible for telling the story that opened the way to God for me. I am not responsible for the way people respond to my story. I am not responsible for dividing people into groups determined by their theology. If our future depends upon the purity of our theology, there is no hope for any of us. All human theology is just that—human. As such it is finite and limited. We see distorted pictures in our theological glass. At the center of my theology is my belief in a God whose grace is wide enough and deep enough for me. I will end with this statement: Whether a person's concept of God comes from Christianity, Islam, Judaism, Hinduism, or some other source, I don't believe in a God who motivates us to hate, destroy, and kill. I believe in the God who loves all people through those who have been changed by the power of the story.

NOTES

[1] Christianity is unlike other religions in that its beliefs are based upon a historical event. Once this position is taken, it becomes subject to the critical scrutiny of historians. Many believers resent the historians, finding refuge in an assertion of scriptural infallibility, thus removing their claim from the realm of historical investigation. Then Christianity becomes similar to Islam, among others. According to Islam, the Koran was dictated to Muhammad in a cave. This is not subject to historical investigation. You either believe it or you don't. However, the fact that a man named Jesus lived in Palestine, that he said certain things and performed certain deeds, that he was crucified under the rule of Pontius Pilate, and that his followers believed they had seen him alive after his death are all valid areas for historical research.

[2] Of all the unfortunate theological positions the Southern Baptist Convention has written into its creed, the removal of the declaration that made Jesus the key to understanding the rest of Scripture is the most egregious. A casual reader of the New Testament will grasp at once that the understanding of the Old Testament by the writers was totally changed by their conviction that God's supreme and most crucial word to humankind had been spoken in Jesus of Nazareth.

[3] See the Epistle to the Ephesians, especially 1:8bff.

[4] As I have observed the prejudiced churches and Christians of our day, I have reminded myself that they are no more prejudiced than those earliest Jewish Christians who resisted the inclusion of Gentiles in the church.